# THE ANALECTS

## CONFUCIUS

INTRODUCTION AND NOTES BY
*John Baldock*

CHARTWELL
BOOKS, INC.

PICTURE CREDITS:
akg-images: 111, 121.
akg-images/Erich Lessing: 37, 43, 47, 53, 59.
akg-images/François Guénet: 33.
Bridgeman Art Library: 9, 65, 73, 80, 90, 99, 104.
clipart.com: 14, 19, 23, 28, 115.
Corbis: 8.

This is an edited version of the original text.

This edition printed in 2010 by
**CHARTWELL BOOKS, INC.**
A Division of **BOOK SALES, INC.**
276 Fifth Avenue Suite 206
New York, New York 10001 USA

Copyright © 2010 Arcturus Publishing Limited
26/27 Bickels Yard, 151–153 Bermondsey Street,
London SE1 3HA

ISBN-13: 978-0-7858-2613-2
ISBN-10: 0-7858-2613-0
AD001350EN

Printed in China

# **CONTENTS**

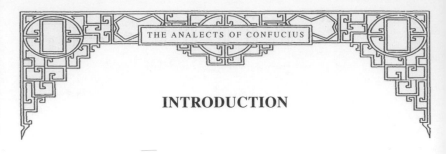

# INTRODUCTION

A contemporary of the Buddha and the Greek philosophers Pythagoras, Xenophanes and Parmenides, Confucius died in 479BCE. Shortly after his death his close followers compiled the collection of his teachings known as the *Lun yü* or *Analects* – a book that has been as widely read in China over the centuries as the Bible has in the West. However, where the Bible explores our relationship with God, the *Analects* concern themselves more with the development of virtue or moral character as a way of ensuring both good government and the self-improvement of the individual.

The *Analects* were first translated into a Western language (Latin) by Matteo Ricci, an Italian Jesuit missionary who travelled to China in 1582. It was either Ricci or his fellow missionary, Michele Ruggieri, who rendered the name of the Chinese philosopher K'ung Ch'iu or K'ung Chung Ni into Latin as 'Confucius'.

## CONFUCIUS

Confucius was born in the state of Lu in 551BCE, in the 22nd year of the reign of Duke Hsian. His father having died when Confucius was only three years old, he was raised in relative poverty by his mother. An early indication of his future path occurred at the age of 15 when, as he recalls in the *Analects*, he set his mind 'upon wisdom' (p.15), studying the traditional rites and the legacy of the rulers of ancient China. He married in 532BCE, aged 19, and in the following year his wife gave birth to their son, Li Po Yü. It was around this time that Confucius began work as a minor official, either for the state or for Duke Chao, first as book-keeper in the grain stores and then as an official in charge of fields and livestock.

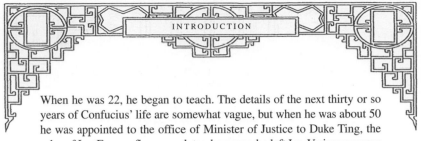

When he was 22, he began to teach. The details of the next thirty or so years of Confucius' life are somewhat vague, but when he was about 50 he was appointed to the office of Minister of Justice to Duke Ting, the ruler of Lu. Four or five years later, however, he left Lu. Various reasons are given for his departure, but it is possible that Confucius left Lu as a matter of principle because he felt he could no longer serve effectively as a minister to Duke Ting. Over the next 13 years (commonly referred to as 'the exile') Confucius visited a number of minor states before being recalled to Lu in 484 or 483BCE during the reign of Duke Ai, the son of Duke Ting. Confucius spent his remaining years teaching and advising Duke Ai and his senior minister, Ch'i Kang Tzu.

The *Analects* themselves offer us numerous insights into the character of Confucius and the way he conducted himself in day-to-day life. He was a modest man, who once described himself as 'a transmitter, not an originator'. He had 'no preconceptions, no predeterminations, no obduracy and no egoism' (p.47). He also refused to make any claims about 'living the noble life' himself or 'being a sage or man of virtue' (p.42). Nonetheless, his profound understanding of human nature and his conviction that the attainment of true wisdom lies open to all who genuinely seek it, whatever their background or social standing, mark him out as one of the most compassionate and influential thinkers in the history of humankind.

## THE ANALECTS

As mentioned above, the principal themes addressed in the *Analects* concern the maintenance of good government and the self-development of the individual. The key to achieving both of these goals is the cultivation of virtue or moral character. It is this which leads Confucius to describe people as either being of a higher or superior type or being lower or inferior. These terms have nothing to do with a person's social or economic status: a higher or superior person is one who has

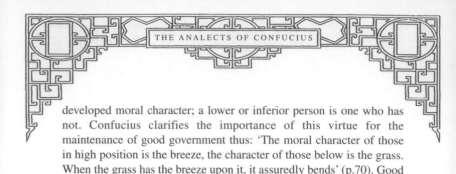

developed moral character; a lower or inferior person is one who has not. Confucius clarifies the importance of this virtue for the maintenance of good government thus: 'The moral character of those in high position is the breeze, the character of those below is the grass. When the grass has the breeze upon it, it assuredly bends' (p.70). Good government also depends on the Mandate of Heaven.

## *Tao*, *te* and the Mandate of Heaven

English translations of the *Analects* contain several references to Heaven – a translation of the Chinese character for *T'ien* – but the word 'Heaven' fails to convey the multidimensional meanings of *T'ien*, such as the sky, the heavens, Nature or the natural order and the Cosmos. An appreciation of these additional meanings is essential for our understanding of the ancient Chinese concept of the Mandate of Heaven (*T'ien Ming*) and of two other words – *Tao* and *te* – which occur frequently in the *Analects* and, like *T'ien*, have more than one meaning. *Tao*, which is generally translated as way, track or path, also denotes the Way (or Will) of Heaven, Nature or the Cosmos. It is to this that Confucius is referring when he asks, 'Why will not men go by the Way?' (p.34). *Te* is usually translated as virtue or moral character, a personal quality which has its source in Heaven and may be acquired by following the Way: 'Fix your mind on the right way [the Way]; hold fast to it in your moral character' (p.38). Despite its celestial source, Confucius stresses the importance of virtue in the everyday life of human beings: 'Virtue is more to man than either water or fire' (p.97).

The concept of the Mandate of Heaven goes back to the legendary first emperors of China and has its roots in the belief that only a truly virtuous person – someone who adheres to the Way – had a right to rule or govern others. As long as the emperor sustained the harmonious relationship between Heaven, Earth and the people, he was said to be in receipt of the Mandate of Heaven. However, if the people rose up against him or the realm suffered misfortune of one kind or another, it

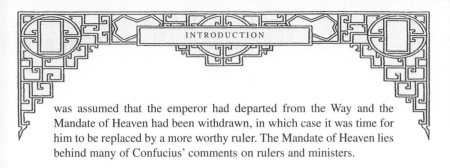
was assumed that the emperor had departed from the Way and the Mandate of Heaven had been withdrawn, in which case it was time for him to be replaced by a more worthy ruler. The Mandate of Heaven lies behind many of Confucius' comments on rulers and ministers.

## Reciprocity and Learning

The principle of reciprocity, which arises several times in the *Analects* and is common to most of the world's spiritual traditions, can be expressed simply as 'consideration for others' – treating other people as we would wish to be treated ourselves. According to Confucius, the key to practising this principle in day-to-day life is 'to be able from one's own self to draw a parallel for the treatment of others' (p.36). Confucius also applied the principle of consideration for others when responding to his disciples' questions, for he tailored his replies to suit the individual disciple's character or needs – for example, the opening paragraphs of Book XII on the meaning of virtue.

When Confucius stresses the importance of learning for the development of moral character, he means learning by observing ourselves and others: 'When you see a man of worth, think how to rise to his level. When you see an unworthy man, then look within and examine yourself' (p.26). Or, as his disciple Tzu Hsia says, 'He who day by day finds out where he is deficient, and who month by month never forgets that in which he has become proficient, may truly be called a lover of learning' (p.116).

Through learning one may also attain wisdom. In some traditions the wise person or sage is portrayed as someone who withdraws from the world to live in seclusion, but this is not the way of Confucius. When asked what constituted wisdom, he replied, 'to devote oneself earnestly to one's duty to humanity' (p.35). It is a definition that is as valid for our modern, westernized world as it was 2,500 years ago in the China of Confucius.

John Baldock

# BOOK I
## CONCERNING FUNDAMENTAL PRINCIPLES

The Master said: 'Is it not indeed a pleasure to acquire knowledge
and constantly to exercise oneself therein? And is it not delightful
to have men of kindred spirit come to one from afar? But is not he
a true philosopher who, though he be unrecognized of men,
cherishes no resentment?'

The philosopher Yu[1] said: 'He who lives a filial life, respecting
the elders, who yet is wishful to give offence to those above him,
is rare; and there has never been any one unwishful to offend
those above him, who has yet been fond of creating disorder. The
true philosopher devotes himself to the fundamentals, for when

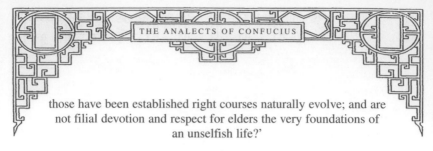

those have been established right courses naturally evolve; and are not filial devotion and respect for elders the very foundations of an unselfish life?'

The Master said: 'Artful speech and an ingratiating demeanour rarely accompany virtue.'

The philosopher Tseng[1] said: 'I daily examine myself on three points – In planning for others have I failed in conscientiousness? In intercourse with friends have I been insincere? And have I failed to practise what I have been taught?'

The Master said: 'To conduct the government of a State of a thousand chariots there must be religious attention to business and good faith, economy in expenditure and love of the people, and their employment on public works at the proper seasons.'

The Master said: 'When a youth is at home let him be filial, when abroad respectful to his elders; let him be circumspect and truthful and, while exhibiting a comprehensive love for all men, let him ally himself with the good. Having so acted, if he have energy to spare, let him employ it in polite studies.'

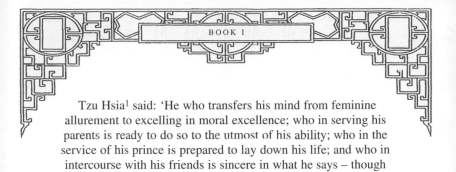

Tzu Hsia[1] said: 'He who transfers his mind from feminine allurement to excelling in moral excellence; who in serving his parents is ready to do so to the utmost of his ability; who in the service of his prince is prepared to lay down his life; and who in intercourse with his friends is sincere in what he says – though others may speak of him as uneducated, I should certainly call him educated.'

The Master said: 'A scholar who is not grave will not inspire respect, and his learning will therefore lack stability. His chief principles should be conscientiousness and sincerity. Let him have no friends unequal to himself. And when in the wrong let him not hesitate to amend.'

The philosopher Tseng said: 'Solicitude on the decease of parents, and the pursuit of this for long after, would cause an abundant restoration of the people's morals.'

Tzu Ch'in[1] inquired of Tzu Kung[1] saying: 'When the Master arrives at any State he always hears about its administration. Does he ask for this information, or, is it tendered to him?'
'The Master,' said Tzu Kung, 'is benign, frank, courteous, temperate, deferential and thus obtains it. The Master's way of asking – how different it is from that of others!'

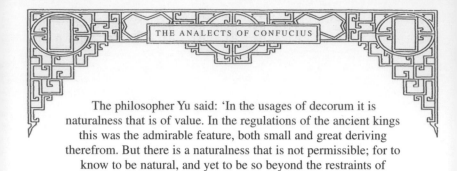
The philosopher Yu said: 'In the usages of decorum it is naturalness that is of value. In the regulations of the ancient kings this was the admirable feature, both small and great deriving therefrom. But there is a naturalness that is not permissible; for to know to be natural, and yet to be so beyond the restraints of decorum is also not permissible.'

The philosopher Yu said: 'When you make a promise consistent with what is right, you can keep your word. When you show respect consistent with good taste, you keep shame and disgrace at a distance. When he in whom you confide is one who does not fail his friends, you may trust him fully.'

The Master said: 'The scholar who in his food does not seek the gratification of his appetite, nor in his dwelling is solicitous of comfort, who is diligent in his work, and guarded in his speech, who associates with the high-principled, and thereby directs himself aright – such a one may really be said to love learning.'

'What do you think,' asked Tzu Kung, 'of the man who is poor yet not servile, or who is rich yet not proud?'
'He will do,' replied the Master, 'but he is not equal to the man who is poor and yet happy, or rich and yet loves courtesy.' Tzu Kung remarked: 'The Ode says this is
Like cutting, then filing;
Like chiselling, then grinding.

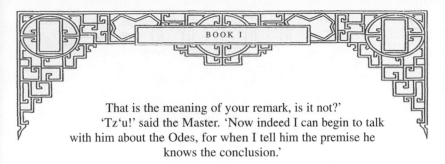

That is the meaning of your remark, is it not?'
'Tz'u!' said the Master. 'Now indeed I can begin to talk
with him about the Odes, for when I tell him the premise he
knows the conclusion.'

The Master said: 'I will not grieve that men do not know me; I
will grieve that I do not know men.'

# BOOK II
## CONCERNING GOVERNMENT

The Master said: 'He who governs by his moral excellence may be compared to the pole-star, which abides in its place, while all the stars bow towards it.'

The Master said: 'Though the Odes number three hundred, one phrase can cover them all, namely, "With purpose undiverted".'[2]

The Master said: 'If you govern the people by laws, and keep

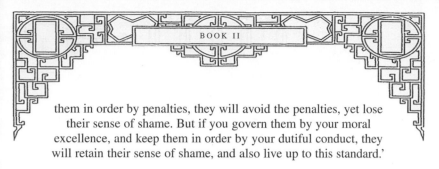

them in order by penalties, they will avoid the penalties, yet lose their sense of shame. But if you govern them by your moral excellence, and keep them in order by your dutiful conduct, they will retain their sense of shame, and also live up to this standard.'

The Master said: 'At fifteen I set my mind upon wisdom. At thirty I stood firm. At forty I was free from doubts. At fifty I understood the laws of Heaven. At sixty my ear was docile. At seventy I could follow the desires of my heart without transgressing the right.'

When Meng I Tzu³ asked what filial duty meant, the Master answered: 'It is not being disobedient.'
Afterwards when Fan Ch'ih⁴ was driving him the Master told him, saying: 'Meng Sun asked me what filial piety meant, and I replied: "Not being disobedient."'
Fan Ch'ih thereupon asked, 'What did you mean?'
The Master answered: 'While parents live serve them rightfully; when they are dead bury them with filial rites, and sacrifice to them with proper ordinances.'

When Meng Wu Po³ asked what filial duty meant the Master answered: 'Parents should only have anxiety when their children are ill.'

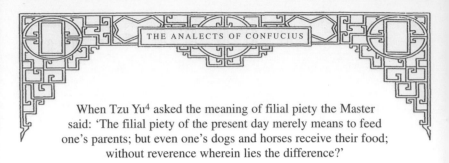

When Tzu Yu[4] asked the meaning of filial piety the Master said: 'The filial piety of the present day merely means to feed one's parents; but even one's dogs and horses receive their food; without reverence wherein lies the difference?'

The Master said: 'I could talk to Hui[4] for a whole day and, as if he were stupid, he never raised an objection; but when he withdrew and I examined into his conduct when not with me, I nevertheless found him fully competent to demonstrate what I had taught him. Hui! he was not stupid.'

The Master said: 'Observe what he does; look into his motives; find out in what he is at peace. Can a man hide himself? Can a man hide himself?'

The Master said: 'He who keeps on reviewing his old and acquiring new knowledge may become a teacher of others.'

The Master said: 'The higher type of man is not a machine.'

On Tzu Kung asking about the nobler type of man the Master said: 'He first practises what he preaches and

afterwards preaches according to his practice.'

The Master said: 'The nobler type of man is broad-minded and not prejudiced. The inferior man is prejudiced and not broad-minded.'

The Master said: 'Learning without thinking is useless. Thinking without learning is dangerous.'

The Master said: 'To devote oneself to irregular speculations is decidedly harmful.'

The Master said: 'Yu! Shall I teach you the meaning of knowledge? When you know a thing to recognize that you know it; and when you do not, to know that you do not know – that is knowledge.'

Tzu Chang[4] was studying with a view to preferment. The Master said to him: 'Hear much, be reserved in what causes you doubt, and speak guardedly of the rest; you will then suffer little criticism. See much, be reserved in what seems imprudent, and act guardedly as to the rest; you will then have few regrets. With

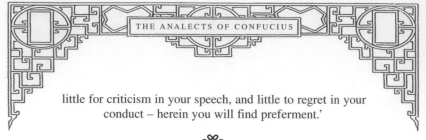

little for criticism in your speech, and little to regret in your conduct – herein you will find preferment.'

Duke Ai[5] inquired saying: 'What should I do to insure the contentment of the people?' 'If you promote the upright and dismiss the ill-doer,' replied Confucius, 'the people will be contented; but if you promote the ill-doer and dismiss the upright, the people will be discontented.'

When Chi K'ang Tzu[6] asked how to inspire the people with respect and loyalty, so that they might be mutually emulous (for the welfare of the state), the Master said: 'Lead them with dignity and they will also be dutiful; be filial and kind and they will be loyal; promote those who excel and teach the incompetent, and they will encourage each other.'

The Master said: 'A man who is without good faith     I do not know how he is to manage! How can a waggon without its yoke-bar for the ox, or a carriage without its collar-bar for the horses, be made to move?'

The Master said: 'To sacrifice to a spirit of an ancestor not one's own is sycophancy. To see the right and not do it is cowardice.'

# BOOK III
## CONCERNING MANNERS AND MORALS

Confucius said of the head of the House of Chi, who had eight
rows of dancers performing in his Temple: 'If he can bear to do
this, what can he not bear to do?'[7]

The Master said: 'A man who is not virtuous, what has he to do
with worship? A man who is not virtuous, what has he to do with
the music of the temple?'

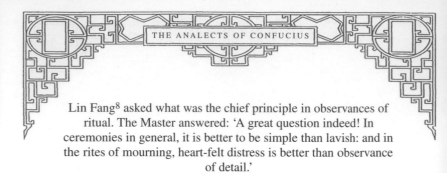

Lin Fang[8] asked what was the chief principle in observances of ritual. The Master answered: 'A great question indeed! In ceremonies in general, it is better to be simple than lavish: and in the rites of mourning, heart-felt distress is better than observance of detail.'

The Master said: 'A gentleman never contends in anything he does – except perhaps in archery. Even then, he bows to his rival and yields him the way as they ascend the pavilion; in like manner he descends and offers him the penalty cup – in his contentions he is still a gentleman.'

Tzu Hsia asked: 'What is the meaning of the passage –
"As she artfully smiles
What dimples appear!
Her bewitching eyes
Show their colours so clear.
Ground spotless and candid
For tracery splendid!"?'
'The painting comes after the ground-work,' answered the Master.
'Then manners are secondary?' said Tzu Hsia.
''Tis Shang [Tzu Hsia] who unfolds my meaning,' replied the Master. 'Now indeed, I can begin to discuss the poets with him.'

He sacrificed to his forefathers as if they were present; he

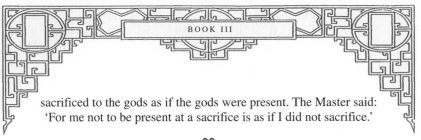

sacrificed to the gods as if the gods were present. The Master said:
'For me not to be present at a sacrifice is as if I did not sacrifice.'

The Master said: 'Chou had the advantage of surveying the two
preceding dynasties. How full was its culture! I follow Chou
dynasty ideas.'9

When the Master first entered the Grand Temple he asked about
everything, whereupon some one remarked: 'Who says the son of
the man of Tsou knows the correct forms? On entering the Grand
Temple he asks about everything.' The Master hearing of it
remarked: 'This too is correct form.'

The Master said: 'In archery piercing the target is not the essential,
for men are not of equal strength. Such was the rule of yore.'

Tzu Kung wished to dispense with the live sheep presented in the
Ducal Temple at the announcement of the new moon. The Master
said: 'T'zu! You care for the sheep. I care for the ritual.'

The Master said: 'If one were to serve one's prince with

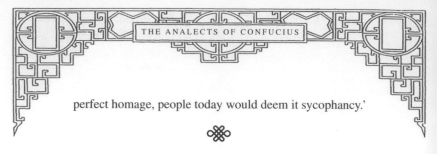
perfect homage, people today would deem it sycophancy.'

When Duke Ting[10] asked how a prince should employ his ministers, and how ministers should serve their prince, Confucius replied saying: 'A prince should employ his ministers with courtesy. A minister should serve his prince with loyalty.'

When Duke Ai asked Tsai Wo[11] concerning the altars to the tutelary deities of the land, Tsai Wo responded: 'The sovereign of Hsia adopted the pine, the men of Yin the cypress, but the men of Chou the chestnut, intimating that the people should stand in dread.' On the Master hearing of this he said: 'When a deed is done it is useless to discuss it, when a thing has taken its course it is useless to remonstrate, what is past and gone it is useless to blame.'

The Master spoke of the Shao music as perfectly beautiful in form and perfectly good in its influence. He spoke of the Wu music as perfectly beautiful in form but not perfectly good in its influence.[12]

The Master said: 'High station filled without magnanimity, religious observances performed without reverence, and "mourning" conducted without grief – from what standpoint shall I view such ways?'

## BOOK IV
### CONCERNING VIRTUE

The Master said: 'It is the moral character of a neighbourhood that constitutes its excellence, and how can he be considered wise who does not elect to dwell in moral surroundings?'

The Master said: 'A man without virtue cannot long abide in adversity, nor can he long abide in happiness; but the virtuous man is at rest in virtue, and the wise man covets it.'

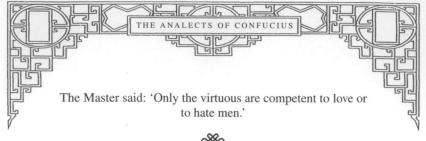

The Master said: 'Only the virtuous are competent to love or to hate men.'

The Master said: 'He who has really set his mind on virtue will do no evil.'

The Master said: 'Wealth and rank are what men desire, but unless they be obtained in the right way they may not be possessed. Poverty and obscurity are what men detest; but unless prosperity be brought about in the right way, they are not to be abandoned. If a man of honour forsakes virtue how is he to fulfil the obligations of his name? A man of honour never disregards virtue, even for the space of a single meal. In moments of haste he cleaves to it; in seasons of peril he cleaves to it.'

The Master said: 'I have never seen one who loved virtue, nor one who hated what was not virtuous. He who loved virtue would esteem nothing above it; and he who hated what is not virtuous would himself be so virtuous that he would allow nothing evil to adhere to him. Is there any one able for a single day to devote his strength to virtue? I have never seen such a one whose ability would be sufficient. If perchance there be such I have never seen him.'

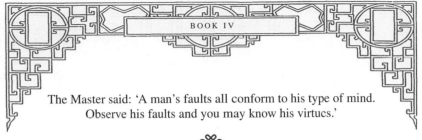

The Master said: 'A man's faults all conform to his type of mind. Observe his faults and you may know his virtues.'

The Master said: 'He who heard the truth in the morning might die content in the evening.'

The Master said: 'The student who aims at wisdom, and yet who is ashamed of shabby clothes and poor food, is not yet worthy to be discoursed with.'

The Master said: 'The wise man in his attitude towards the world has neither predilections nor prejudices. He is on the side of what is right.'

The Master said: 'The man of honour thinks of his character, the inferior man of his position. The man of honour desires justice, the inferior man favour.'

The Master said: 'He who works for his own interests will arouse much animosity.'

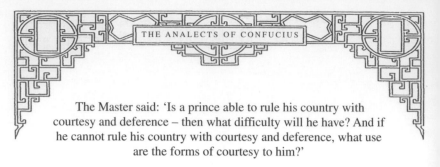
The Master said: 'Is a prince able to rule his country with courtesy and deference – then what difficulty will he have? And if he cannot rule his country with courtesy and deference, what use are the forms of courtesy to him?'

The Master said: 'One should not be concerned at lack of position, but should be concerned about what will fit him to occupy it. One should not be concerned at being unknown, but should seek to be worthy of being known.'

The Master said: 'Shen! My teaching contains one all-pervading principle.' 'Yes,' replied Tseng Tzu. When the Master had left the room the disciples asked, 'What did he mean?' Tseng Tzu replied, 'Our Master's teaching is simply this: Conscientiousness within and consideration for others.'

The Master said: 'The wise man is informed in what is right. The inferior man is informed in what will pay.'

The Master said: 'When you see a man of worth, think how to rise to his level. When you see an unworthy man, then look within and examine yourself.'

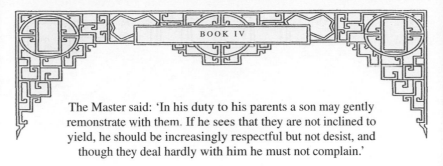

The Master said: 'In his duty to his parents a son may gently remonstrate with them. If he sees that they are not inclined to yield, he should be increasingly respectful but not desist, and though they deal hardly with him he must not complain.'

The Master said: 'The age of one's parents should ever be kept in mind, as an occasion at once for joy and for fear.'

The Master said: 'The men of old were reserved in speech out of shame lest they should come short in deed.'

The Master said: 'The self-restrained seldom err.'

The Master said: 'The wise man desires to be slow to speak but quick to act.'

The Master said: 'Virtue never dwells alone; it always has neighbours.'

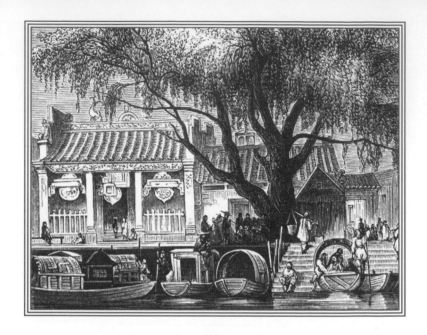

# BOOK V
## CONCERNING CERTAIN DISCIPLES AND OTHERS[13]

The Master said of Kung Yeh Ch'ang that he was a suitable man
to marry, for though he had been in prison it was through no
wrong-doing of his. So he gave him his own daughter to wife. The
Master said of Nan Yung that when the country was well governed
he would not be set aside, and when the country was ill
governed he would escape suffering and death. So he gave
him his elder brother's daughter to wife.

The Master said of Tzu Chien: 'An honourable man
indeed is such a one as he! Were the state of Lu without

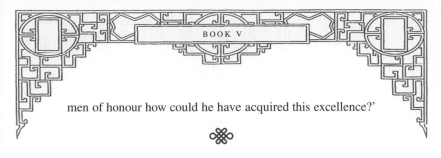

men of honour how could he have acquired this excellence?'

Some one remarked: 'A virtuous man is Yung, but he is not ready of speech.' 'What need has he of ready speech?' said the Master. 'The man who is always ready with his tongue to others will often be disliked by them. I do not know about his virtue, but what need has he of ready speech?'

The Master wanted to engage Ch'i-tiao K'ai in office, but he replied: 'I still lack confidence for this.' Whereat the Master was pleased.

The Master said: 'My doctrines make no progress. I will get me on a raft and float away upon the sea! If any one accompanies me will it not be Yu?' Tzu Lu [Yu] on hearing this was pleased; whereupon the Master said: 'Yu is fonder of daring than I; he also exercises no discretion.'

The Master addressing Tzu Kung said: 'Which is the superior, you or Hui?' 'How dare I look at Hui?' he answered; 'Hui hears one point and from it apprehends the whole ten. I hear one point and apprehend a second therefrom.' The Master said: 'You are not equal to him, I grant you, you are not equal to him.'

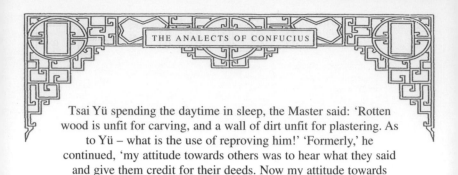

Tsai Yü spending the daytime in sleep, the Master said: 'Rotten wood is unfit for carving, and a wall of dirt unfit for plastering. As to Yü – what is the use of reproving him!' 'Formerly,' he continued, 'my attitude towards others was to hear what they said and give them credit for their deeds. Now my attitude towards others is to listen to what they say and note what they do. It is through Yü that I have made this change.'

The Master said: 'I have never seen a man of strong character.' Some one remarked, 'There is Shen Ch'eng.' 'Ch'eng!' said the Master. 'He is under the influence of his passions, and how can he be possessed of strength of character?'

Tzu Kung said: 'What I do not wish others to do to me, that also I wish not to do to them.' 'Tzu!' observed the Master, 'that is a point to which you have not attained.'

Tzu Kung said: 'Our Master's culture and refinement all may hear; but our Master's discourse on the nature of man and the laws of heaven it is not given to all to hear.'

When Tzu Lu heard any precept and had not yet been able to put

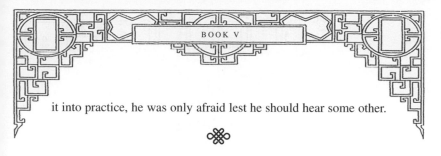
it into practice, he was only afraid lest he should hear some other.

Tzu Kung asked: 'On what ground has K'ung Tzu[14] received his posthumous title of Wen?'
'He was clever and fond of learning,' replied the Master, 'and he was not ashamed to seek knowledge from his inferiors – that is why he has been styled "Cultured".'

The Master remarked of Tzu Ch'an[15] that he had four of the Ideal Man's characteristics – in his personal conduct he was serious, in his duty to his superior he was deferential, in providing for the people he was beneficent, and in directing them he was just.

The Master said: 'Yen P'ing Chung was gifted in the art of friendship. Whatever the lapse of time, he maintained towards his friends the same consideration.'

The Master said: 'Tsang Wen Chung kept a large tortoise in an edifice, on whose pillar-tops were representations of hills, and on its king-posts of water plants – of what sort was his wisdom?'

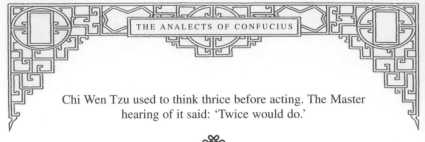
Chi Wen Tzu used to think thrice before acting. The Master hearing of it said: 'Twice would do.'

The Master said: 'While good order prevailed in his state, Ning Wu Tzu was a wise man. When the state fell into disorder, he was a fool. His wisdom may be equalled, his folly cannot be equalled.'

Once when Yen Yüan and Tzu Lu were standing by him the Master said: 'Suppose each of you tells his wishes?' 'I should like,' said Tzu Lu, 'to have carriages and horses and light furs to wear, so as to share them with my friends, nor would I feel any annoyance if they spoilt them.' 'I should like,' said Yen Yüan, 'never to make a display of my good qualities, nor a parade of my merits.' 'May we hear the Master's wishes?' asked Tzu Lu. 'They would be,' said the Master, 'to comfort the aged, be faithful to my friends, and cherish the young.'

The Master said: 'It is all in vain! I have never yet seen a man who could perceive his own faults and bring the charge home against himself.'

The Master said: 'Even in a hamlet of ten houses there must be men as conscientious and sincere as myself, but none as fond of learning as I am.'

# BOOK VI
## CONCERNING CERTAIN DISCIPLES AND OTHER SUBJECTS

Duke Ai asked which of the disciples was fond of learning.
Confucius answered him: 'There was Yen Hui – he was fond of
learning; he never visited his anger on another, and he never
repeated a fault. Unfortunately his life was short and he died
Now there is none like him, nor have I heard of one who is
fond of learning.'

The Master said, 'Hui! His heart for three months together
never departed from virtue. As to the others, on some day

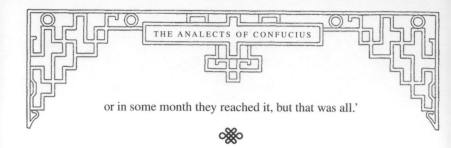
or in some month they reached it, but that was all.'

The Master said: 'What a man of worth was Hui! A single bamboo bowl of millet; a single ladle of cabbage soup; living in a mean alley! Others could not have borne his distress, but Hui never abated his cheerfulness. What a worthy man was Hui!'

Jan Ch'iu[16] remarked: 'It is not that I have no pleasure in your teaching, Sir, but I am not strong enough.' 'He who is not strong enough,' answered the Master, 'gives up half way, but you are drawing the line already.'

The Master speaking to Tzu Hsia said: 'Be you a scholar of the nobler type, not a scholar of the inferior man's type.'

The Master said: 'Who can go forth except by the Door? Why will not men go by the Way?'

The Master said: 'When nature exceeds training, you have the rustic. When training exceeds nature, you have the clerk. It is only when nature and training are proportionately

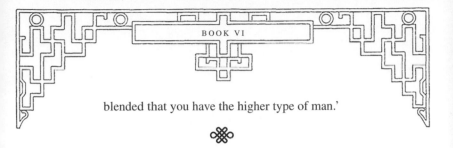

blended that you have the higher type of man.'

The Master said: 'Man is born for uprightness. Without it he is lucky to escape with his life!'

The Master said: 'He who knows the truth is not equal to him who loves it, and he who loves it is not equal to him who delights in it.'

The Master said: 'To men above the average one may discourse on higher things; but to those who are below the average one may not discourse on higher things.'

When Fan Ch'ih asked what constituted wisdom the Master replied: 'To devote oneself earnestly to one's duty to humanity and, while respecting the spirits of the departed, to avoid them, may be called wisdom.'
On his asking about virtue, the Master replied: 'The man of virtue puts duty first, however difficult, and makes what he will gain thereby an after consideration – and this may be called virtue.'

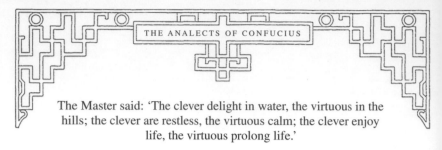
The Master said: 'The clever delight in water, the virtuous in the hills; the clever are restless, the virtuous calm; the clever enjoy life, the virtuous prolong life.'

Tsai Wo asked, saying: 'An altruist, even if some one said to him, "There is a man in the well," would, I suppose, go in after him?' 'Why should he act like that?' answered the Master. 'The higher type of man might hasten to the well, but not precipitate himself into it; he might be imposed upon, but not utterly hoodwinked.'

Tzu Kung said: 'Suppose there was one who conferred benefits far and wide upon the people, and who was able to succour the multitude, what might one say of him? Could he be called a philanthropist?'
'What has he to do with philanthropy?' said the Master. 'Must he not be a sage? Even Yao and Shun[17] felt their deficiency herein. For the philanthropist is one who desiring to maintain himself sustains others, and desiring to develop himself develops others. To be able from one's own self to draw a parallel for the treatment of others – that may be called the rule of philanthropy.'

# BOOK VII
## CONCERNING THE MASTER HIMSELF

The Master said: 'The meditative treasuring up of knowledge, the unwearying pursuit of wisdom, the tireless instruction of others which of these is found in me?'

The Master said: 'Neglect in the cultivation of character, lack of thoroughness in study, incompetency to move towards recognized duty, inability to correct my imperfections – these are what cause me solicitude.'

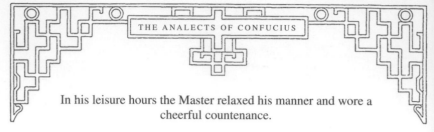

In his leisure hours the Master relaxed his manner and wore a cheerful countenance.

The Master said: 'How utterly fallen off I am! For long I have not dreamed as of yore that I saw the Duke [Wen] of Chou.'

The Master said: 'Fix your mind on the right way; hold fast to it in your moral character; follow it up in kindness to others; take your recreation in the polite arts.'

The Master said: 'I expound nothing to him who is not earnest, nor help out any one not anxious to express himself. When I have demonstrated one angle and he cannot bring me back the other three, then I do not repeat my lesson.'

When the Master dined by the side of a mourner he never ate to the full. On the same day that he had been mourning he never sang.

The Master addressing Yen Yüan said: 'To accept office when required, and to dwell in retirement when set aside – only you and I have this spirit.'
'But suppose,' said Tzu Lu, 'that the Master had the conduct of the

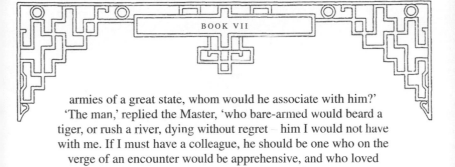

armies of a great state, whom would he associate with him?'
'The man,' replied the Master, 'who bare-armed would beard a
tiger, or rush a river, dying without regret — him I would not have
with me. If I must have a colleague, he should be one who on the
verge of an encounter would be apprehensive, and who loved
strategy and its successful issue.'

The Master said: 'If wealth were a thing one could count on
finding, even though it meant my becoming a whip-holding
groom, I would do it. As one cannot count on finding it, I will
follow the quests that I love better.'

The subjects which the Master treated with great solicitude were –
fasting, war, and disease.

When the Master was in Ch'i he heard the Shao music and for
three months was unconscious of the taste of meat. 'I did not
imagine,' said he, 'that music had reached such perfection as this.'

The Master said: 'With coarse food to eat, water for drink, and a bent
arm for a pillow – even in such a state I could be happy, for wealth
and honour obtained unworthily are to me as a fleeting cloud.'

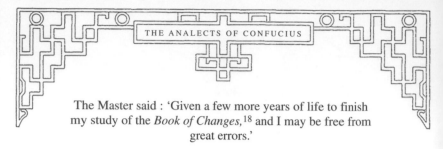

The Master said : 'Given a few more years of life to finish my study of the *Book of Changes*,[18] and I may be free from great errors.'

The subjects on which the Master most frequently discoursed were – the Odes, the History, and the observances of the Rites – on all these he constantly dwelt.

The Duke of She asked Tzu Lu what he thought about Confucius, but Tzu Lu returned him no answer. 'Why did you not say,' said the Master, 'he is simply a man so eager for improvement that he forgets his food, so happy therein that he forgets his sorrows, and so does not observe that old age is at hand?'

The Master said: 'I am not one who has innate knowledge, but one who, loving antiquity, is diligent in seeking it therein.'

The Master would not discuss prodigies, prowess, lawlessness, or the supernatural.

The Master said: 'When walking in a party of three, my teachers are always present. I can select the good qualities of the one and

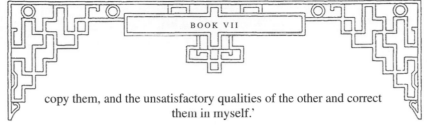

copy them, and the unsatisfactory qualities of the other and correct
them in myself.'

The Master took four subjects for his teaching – culture, conduct,
conscientiousness, and good faith.

The Master said: 'It is not mine to see an inspired man. Could I
behold a noble man, I would be content.'
The Master said: 'It is not mine to see a really good man. Could I
see a man of constant purpose, I would be content. Affecting to
have when they have not, empty yet affecting to be full, in straits
yet affecting to be prosperous – how hard it is for such men to
have constancy of purpose!'

The Master fished with a line, but not with a net; when shooting he
did not aim at a resting bird.

The Master said: 'There are men, probably, who do things
correctly without knowing the reason why, but I am not like
that: I hear much, select the good and follow it; I see much and
treasure it up. This is the next best thing to philosophical
knowledge.'

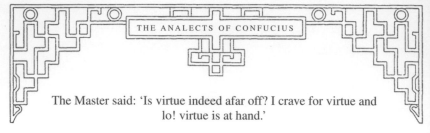
The Master said: 'Is virtue indeed afar off? I crave for virtue and lo! virtue is at hand.'

The Master said: 'In literature perhaps I may compare with others, but as to my living the noble life, to that I have not yet attained.'

The Master said: 'As to being a sage, or a man of virtue, how dare I presume to such a claim? But as to striving thereafter unwearyingly, and teaching others therein without flagging – that can be said of me, and that is all.'
'And that,' said Kung-hsi Hua,[19] 'is just what we disciples cannot learn.'

The Master said: 'Men, if prodigal, are uncontrolled; if frugal then narrow: but better be narrow than uncontrolled.'

The Master said: 'The noble man is calm and serene, the inferior man is continually worried and anxious.'

The Master was affable yet dignified, commanding yet not overbearing, courteous yet easy.

# BOOK VIII
## CHIEFLY CONCERNING CERTAIN ANCIENT WORTHIES

The Master said: 'T'ai Po may be described as possessing a character of the noblest. He resolutely renounced the imperial throne, leaving people no ground for appreciating his conduct.'

The Master said: 'Courtesy uncontrolled by the laws of good taste becomes laboured effort, caution uncontrolled becomes timidity, boldness uncontrolled becomes recklessness, and frankness uncontrolled becomes effrontery. When the highly placed pay generous regard to their own families, the people are equally

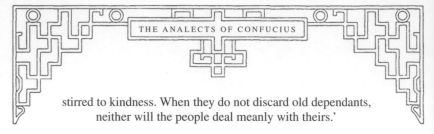
stirred to kindness. When they do not discard old dependants, neither will the people deal meanly with theirs.'

During Tseng Tzu's illness Meng Ching Tzu[20] called to make inquiries. Tseng Tzu spoke to him saying: 'When a bird is dying, its song is sad. When a man is dying, what he says is worth listening to. The three rules of conduct upon which a man of high rank should place value are – in his bearing to avoid rudeness and remissness, in ordering his looks to aim at sincerity, and in the tone of his conversation to keep aloof from vulgarity and impropriety. As to the details of temple vessels – there are proper officers for looking after them.'

Tseng Tzu said: 'Talented, yet seeking knowledge from the untalented; of many attainments, yet seeking knowledge from those with few; having, as though he had not; full, yet bearing himself as if empty; offended against, yet not retaliating – once upon a time I had a friend who lived after this manner.'

Tseng Tzu said: 'The scholar must not be without capacity and fortitude, for his load is heavy and the road is long. He takes virtue for his load, and is not that heavy? Only with death does his course end, and is not that long?'

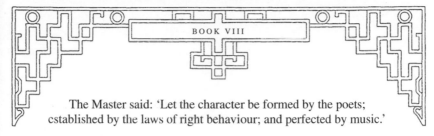

BOOK VIII

The Master said: 'Let the character be formed by the poets; established by the laws of right behaviour; and perfected by music.'

The Master said: 'The people may be made to follow a course but not to understand the reason why.'

The Master said: 'Love of daring and resentment of poverty drive men to desperate deeds; and men who lack moral character, if resentment of them be carried too far, will be driven to similar deeds.'

The Master said: 'If a man has gifts as admirable as those of Duke Chou [King Wen], yet be vain and mean, his other gifts are unworthy of notice.'

The Master said: 'It is not easy to find a man who has studied for three years without aiming at pay.'

The Master said: 'The man of unwavering sincerity and love of moral discipline will keep to the death his excellent principles. He will not enter a tottering state nor dwell in a rebellious one. When law and order prevail in the empire, he is in evidence. When it is without law and order, he withdraws. When law and order prevail

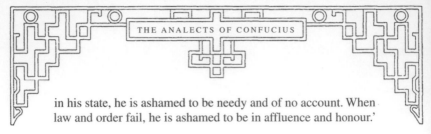
in his state, he is ashamed to be needy and of no account. When law and order fail, he is ashamed to be in affluence and honour.'

The Master said: 'He who does not occupy the office does not discuss its policy.'

The Master said: 'With the impulsive yet evasive, the simple yet dishonest, the stupid yet untruthful, I hold no acquaintance.'

The Master said: 'Learn as if you were not reaching your goal, and as though you were afraid of missing it.'

The Master said: 'How sublime the way Shun and Yü[21] undertook the empire, and yet as if it were nothing to them!'

The Master said: 'In Yü I can find no room for criticism. Simple in his own food and drink, he was unsparing in his filial offerings to the spirits. Shabby in his workaday clothes he was most scrupulous as to the elegance of his kneeling-apron and sacrificial crown. Humble as to the character of his palace, he spent his strength in the draining and ditching of the country. In Yü I find no room for criticism.'

# BOOK IX
## CHIEFLY PERSONAL

The Master seldom spoke on profit, on the orderings of
Providence, and on perfection.

The Master was entirely free from four things: he had no
preconceptions, no predeterminations, no obduracy, and no egoism.

When the Master was in jeopardy in K'uang, he said, 'Since King
Wen is no longer alive, does not the mantle of enlightenment (*wen*)

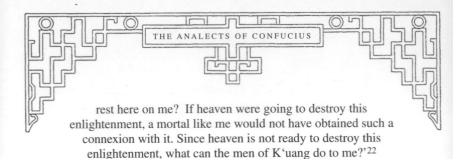
rest here on me? If heaven were going to destroy this enlightenment, a mortal like me would not have obtained such a connexion with it. Since heaven is not ready to destroy this enlightenment, what can the men of K'uang do to me?'[22]

A great minister inquired of Tzu Kung saying, 'Your Master – he is surely inspired? What varied acquirements he has!' Tzu Kung answered, 'Of a truth Heaven has lavishly endowed him, to the point of inspiration, and his acquirements are also many.'
When the Master heard of it, he said: 'Does the minister really know me? In my youth I was in humble circumstances, and for that reason gained a variety of acquirements – in common matters: but does nobleness of character depend on variety? It does not depend on variety.'
Lao[23] said, 'The Master used to say, "I have not been occupied in official life, and so have had time to become acquainted with the arts!"'

The Master said : 'Am I indeed a man with innate knowledge? I have no such knowledge; but when an uncultivated person, in all simplicity, comes to me with a question, I thrash out its pros and cons until I fathom it.'

Yen Yüan heaved a deep sigh and said: 'The more I look up at It, the higher It rises. The more I probe It, the more impenetrable It becomes. I catch a glimpse of It in front, and It is instantly behind.

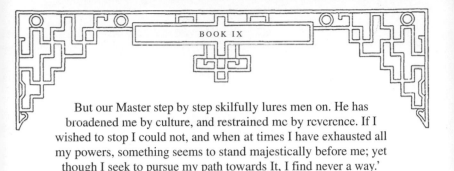

But our Master step by step skilfully lures men on. He has broadened me by culture, and restrained me by reverence. If I wished to stop I could not, and when at times I have exhausted all my powers, something seems to stand majestically before me; yet though I seek to pursue my path towards It, I find never a way.'

Tzu Kung asked : 'If I had a lovely jewel here, should I shut it up in a casket and keep it, or seek a good price and sell it?' 'By all means sell it! Sell it!' answered the Master – 'But I myself would wait for a good offer.'[24]

The Master proposed to go and dwell among the nine uncivilized tribes of the east; whereupon some one remarked: 'But they are so uncivilized, how can you do that?' The Master responded, 'Were a man of noble character to dwell among them, what lack of civilization would there be?'

The Master said: 'It was only after my return from Wei to Lu that music was revised, and that the secular and sacred pieces were properly differentiated.'

The Master said: 'In public life to do my duty to my prince or minister; in private life to do my duty to my fathers and brethren; in my duties to the departed never daring to be otherwise than

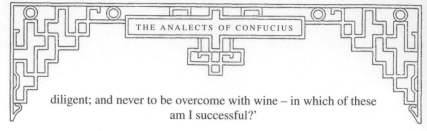

diligent; and never to be overcome with wine – in which of these am I successful?'

Once when the Master was standing by a stream he observed: 'All is transient, like this! Unceasing day and night!'

The Master said: 'I have never yet seen a man whose love of virtue equalled his love of woman.'

The Master said: 'Suppose I am raising a mound, and, while it is still unfinished by a basketful, I stop short, it is I that stops short. Or, suppose I begin on the level ground – although I throw down but one basketful, and continue to do so, then it is I that makes progress.'

The Master said: 'Ah! Hui was the one to whom I could tell things and who never failed to attend to them.'

The Master, referring to Yen Yüan [Hui], said: 'Alas! I ever saw him make progress, and never saw him stand still.'

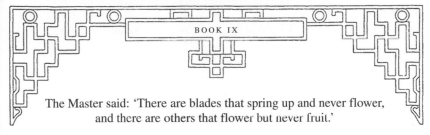

The Master said: 'There are blades that spring up and never flower, and there are others that flower but never fruit.'

The Master said: 'Can any one refuse assent to words of just admonition? But it is amendment that is of value. Can any one be otherwise than pleased with advice persuasively offered? But it is the application that is of value. Mere interest without application, mere assent without amendment – I can do nothing whatever with men of such calibre.'

The Master said: 'Make conscientiousness and sincerity your leading principles. Have no friends inferior to yourself. And when in the wrong, do not hesitate to amend.'

The Master said: 'You may rob a three corps army of its commander-in-chief, but you cannot rob even a common man of his will.'

The Master said: 'Wearing a shabby, hemp-quilted robe, and standing by others dressed in fox and badger, yet in no way abashed – Yu [Tzu Lu] would be the one for that, eh? Unfriendly to none, and courting none, what does he that is not excellent?' As Tzu Lu afterwards was perpetually intoning this, the Master

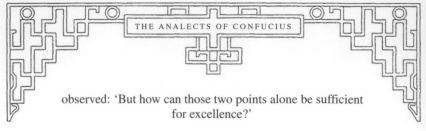

observed: 'But how can those two points alone be sufficient
for excellence?'

The Master said: 'Only when the year grows cold do we realize
that the pine and the cypress are the last to fade.'

The Master said: 'The enlightened are free from doubt, the
virtuous from anxiety, and the brave from fear.'

The Master said: 'There are some with whom one can associate in
study, but who are not yet able to make common advance towards
the truth: there are others who can make common advance towards
the truth, but who are not yet able to take with you a like firm
stand; and there are others with whom you can take such a firm
stand, but with whom you cannot associate in judgement.'

# BOOK X
## CONCERNING THE SAGE IN HIS DAILY LIFE

Confucius in his native village bore himself with simplicity, as if
he had no gifts of speech. But when in the temple or at court,
he expressed himself readily and clearly, yet with a measure
of reserve.

At court, when conversing with ministers of his own rank, he
spoke out boldly; when conversing with the higher ministers
he spoke respectfully; but when the prince was present, his
movements were nervous, though self-possessed.

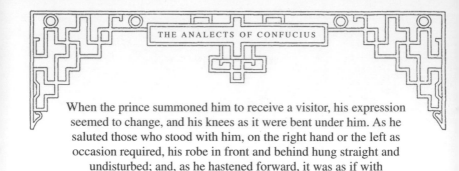
When the prince summoned him to receive a visitor, his expression seemed to change, and his knees as it were bent under him. As he saluted those who stood with him, on the right hand or the left as occasion required, his robe in front and behind hung straight and undisturbed; and, as he hastened forward, it was as if with outstretched wings.

When the visitor had departed he always reported, saying, 'The Guest is no longer looking back at us.'

On entering the palace gate he appeared to stoop, as though the gate were not high enough to admit him. He never stood in the middle of the gateway, nor in going through did he step on the sill. As he passed the throne he wore a constrained expression, his knees appeared to bend, and words seemed to fail him. As he ascended the audience hall, holding up his skirt, he appeared to stoop, and he held his breath as if he dare not breathe. On coming forth from his audience, after descending the first step, his expression relaxed into one of relief; at the bottom of the steps he hastened forward as with outstretched wings, and on regaining his place he maintained an attitude of nervous respect.

He carried the ducal mace with bent back, as if unequal to its weight, neither higher than when making a bow, nor lower than when offering a gift: his expression, too, was perturbed and anxious, and he dragged his feet as if something were trailing behind.

While offering the presents with which he was commissioned he

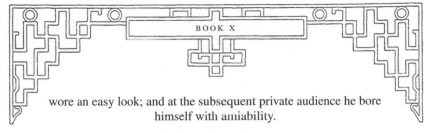

wore an easy look; and at the subsequent private audience he bore
himself with amiability.

He did not wear facings of purple or mauve, nor even in undress
did he use red or crimson. In the hot weather he wore an unlined
gown of fine or loose woven material, but always outside and over
another. With a black robe he wore black lambskin, with a light
robe fawn, and with a yellow robe fox. His undress fur gown was
long, with the right sleeve cut short. He always had his sleeping-
garment made half as long again as his body. He had thick fox or
badger for home wear. When out of mourning he omitted none of
the usual ornaments. His skirts, all save his court skirt, he always
shaped towards the waist. He did not pay visits of condolence in
dark lamb's fur or a dark hat. At the new moon he always put on
his court robes and presented himself at court.

When fasting he always wore a spotless suit of linen cloth. When
fasting, too, he always altered his diet, and in his dwelling always
changed his seat.

He had no objection to his rice being of the finest, nor to having
his meat finely minced. Rice affected by the weather, or turned, he
would not eat, nor fish that was unsound, nor flesh that was
tainted. Neither would he eat anything discoloured, nor that smelt,
nor that was under- or over-cooked, or not in season. He would not
eat anything improperly cut, nor anything served without its proper

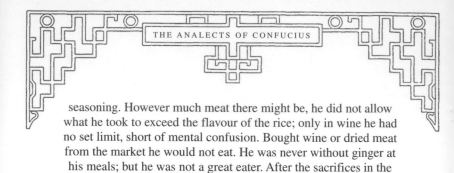
seasoning. However much meat there might be, he did not allow what he took to exceed the flavour of the rice; only in wine he had no set limit, short of mental confusion. Bought wine or dried meat from the market he would not eat. He was never without ginger at his meals; but he was not a great eater. After the sacrifices in the ducal temple he never kept his share of the flesh overnight, nor the flesh of his ancestral sacrifices more than three days, lest after three days it might not be eaten. He did not converse while eating, nor talk when in bed. Though his food were only coarse rice and vegetable broth, he invariably offered a little in sacrifice, and always with solemnity.

He would not sit on his mat unless it were straight.

When his fellow villagers had a feast he only left after the elders had departed. When his fellow villagers held a procession to expel the pestilential influences, he put on his court robes and stood on the eastern steps.

When sending complimentary inquiries to any one in another state, he bowed twice as he escorted his messenger forth. On K'ang Tzu[25] sending him a present of medicine he bowed and accepted it, but said: 'As I am not well acquainted with it, I do not dare to taste it.'

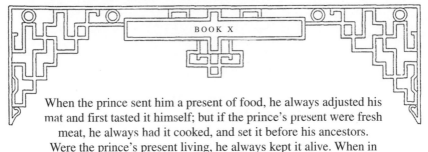

When the prince sent him a present of food, he always adjusted his mat and first tasted it himself; but if the prince's present were fresh meat, he always had it cooked, and set it before his ancestors. Were the prince's present living, he always kept it alive. When in attendance on the prince at a state dinner, while the prince sacrificed he acted the subordinate part of first tasting the dishes. When he was ill and the prince came to see him, he had his head laid to the east, and his court robes thrown over him, with his sash drawn across. When his prince commanded his presence, he did not wait while his carriage was being yoked, but started on foot.

On entering the imperial Ancestral Temple, he asked about every detail.

When a friend died, with no one to see to the rites, he would say, 'I will see to his funeral.' On receiving a present from a friend, unless it were sacrificial flesh, he never made obeisance, not even if it were a carriage and horses.

In bed he did not lie like a corpse. At home he wore no formal air. Whenever he saw any one in mourning, even though it were an intimate acquaintance, his expression always changed, and when he saw any one in a cap of state, or a blind man, even though not in public, he always showed respect. On meeting any one in deep mourning, he would bow to the crossbar of his carriage, as he did also to any one carrying the census boards. When entertained at a

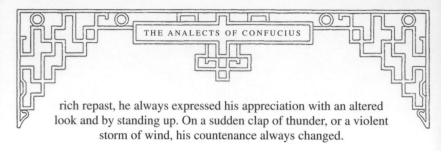
rich repast, he always expressed his appreciation with an altered look and by standing up. On a sudden clap of thunder, or a violent storm of wind, his countenance always changed.

When mounting his carriage he always stood correctly, holding the mounting-cord in his hand. In the carriage he did not look behind, nor speak hastily, nor point with his hands.

# BOOK XI
## CHIEFLY CONCERNING THE DISCIPLES

The Master observed: 'In the arts of civilization our forerunners
are esteemed uncultivated, while in those arts, their successors are
looked upon as cultured gentlemen. But when I have need of those
arts, I follow our forerunners.'

The Master said: 'Of all who were with me in Ch'en and Ch'ai,
not one now comes to my door.'[26]
Noted for moral character there were Yen Yüan, Min Tzu Ch'ien,
Jan Niu and Chung Kung; for gifts of speech Tsai Wo and
Tzu Kung; for administrative ability Jan Yu and Chi Lu

[Tzu Lu]; and for literature and learning Tzu Yu and Tzu Hsia.

The Master said: 'Hui was not one who gave me any assistance. He was invariably satisfied with whatever I said.'

The Master said: 'What a filial son Min Tzu Ch'ien has been! No one takes exception to what his parents and brothers have said of him!'

When Yen Yüan died the Master said: 'Alas! Heaven has bereft me; Heaven has bereft me.'

When Yen Yüan died the Master bewailed him with exceeding grief, whereupon his followers said to him, 'Sir! You are carrying your grief to excess.'
'Have I gone to excess?' asked he. 'But if I may not grieve exceedingly over this man, for whom shall I grieve?'

When Yen Hui [Yen Yüan] died the other disciples proposed to give him an imposing funeral, to which the Master said: 'It will not do.' Nevertheless they buried him with pomp.

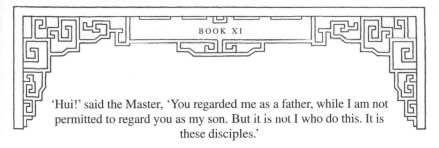

'Hui!' said the Master, 'You regarded me as a father, while I am not permitted to regard you as my son. But it is not I who do this. It is these disciples.'

When Chi Lu asked about his duty to the spirits the Master replied: 'While still unable to do your duty to the living, how can you do your duty to the dead?'
When he ventured to ask about death, Confucius answered: 'Not yet understanding life, how can you understand death?'

Once when Min Tzu was standing by the Master's side he looked so self-reliant, Tzu Lu so full of energy, and Jan Yu and Tzu Kung so frank and fearless that the Master was highly gratified.
'But,' said he, 'a man like Yu will not come to a natural death.'[27]

When the men of Lu were for rebuilding the Long Treasury, Min Tzu Ch'ien observed, 'How would it do to restore it as before? Why need it be reconstructed?' The Master said: 'This man seldom speaks, but when he does he is sure to hit the mark.'

Tzu Kung asked which was the better, Shih or Shang?[28] The Master replied: 'Shih exceeds, Shang comes short.'
'So then,' queried he, 'Shih surpasses Shang, eh?'

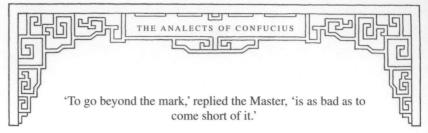

'To go beyond the mark,' replied the Master, 'is as bad as to come short of it.'

Ch'ai was simple-minded; Shen dull; Shih shallow; Yu unrefined.[29]

The Master said: 'Hui! he was almost perfect, yet he was often in want. T'zu[30] was not content with his lot, and yet his goods increased abundantly; nevertheless in his judgements he often hit the mark.'

When Tzu Chang asked what characterized the way of the man of natural goodness, the Master replied: 'He does not tread the beaten track, nor yet does he enter into the inner sanctum of philosophy.'

The Master said: 'That a man's address may be solid and reliable, this one may grant; but does it follow that he is a man of the higher type, or is his seriousness only in appearance?'

When Tzu Lu asked whether he should put what he heard into immediate practice, the Master answered, 'You have parents and elders still living, why should you at once put all you hear into practice?'

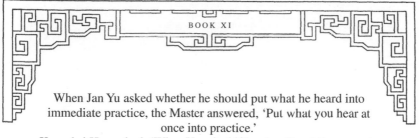

When Jan Yu asked whether he should put what he heard into
immediate practice, the Master answered, 'Put what you hear at
once into practice.'

Kung-hsi Hua asked: 'When Yu asked if he should put the precepts
he heard into immediate practice, you, Sir, replied, "You have
parents and elders alive"; but when Ch'iu asked if he should put
the precepts he heard into immediate practice, you, Sir, replied,
"Put what you hear at once into practice." As I am perplexed about
your meaning I venture to ask a solution.'

'Ch'iu,' answered the Master, 'lags behind, so I urged him
forward; but Yu has energy for two men, so I held him back.'

When the Master was put in peril in K'uang, Yen Hui
fell behind. On the Master saying to him, 'I thought you were
dead,' he replied, 'While you, Sir, live, how should I dare to die?'

When Chi Tzu-jan[31] asked if Chung Yu and Jan Ch'iu could be
called great ministers, the Master replied, 'I thought, Sir, you were
going to ask about something extraordinary, and it is only a
question about Yu and Ch'iu. He who may be called a great
minister is one who serves his prince according to the right, and
when that cannot be, resigns. Now, as for Yu and Ch'iu, they may
be styled ordinary ministers.'

'So, then,' said Tzu Jan, 'they would follow their chief, eh?'

'A parricide or regicide,' answered the Master, 'they would
assuredly not follow, however.'

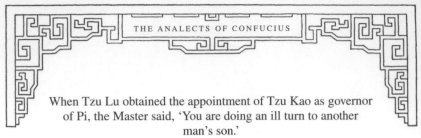

When Tzu Lu obtained the appointment of Tzu Kao as governor of Pi, the Master said, 'You are doing an ill turn to another man's son.'

'He will have his people and officers,' replied Tzu Lu, 'he will also have the altars of the land and the grain, why must he read books before he is considered educated?'

'It is because of this kind of talk,' said the Master, 'that I hate glib people.'

# BOOK XII
## CONCERNING VIRTUE, NOBILITY, AND POLITY

When Yen Yüan asked the meaning of virtue, the Master replied:
'Virtue is the denial of self and response to what is right and
proper. Deny yourself for one day and respond to the right and
proper, and everybody will accord you virtuous. For has virtue its
source in oneself, or is it forsooth derived from others?'
'May I beg for the main features?' asked Yen Yüan. The Master
answered: 'When wrong and improper do not look, when wrong
and improper do not listen, when wrong and improper do not
speak, when wrong and improper do not move.'
'Though I am not clever,' said Yen Yüan, 'permit me to carry out
these precepts.'

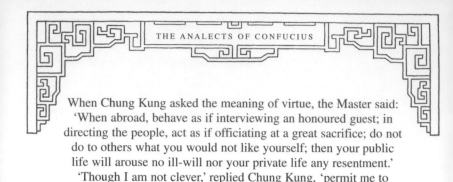

When Chung Kung asked the meaning of virtue, the Master said: 'When abroad, behave as if interviewing an honoured guest; in directing the people, act as if officiating at a great sacrifice; do not do to others what you would not like yourself; then your public life will arouse no ill-will nor your private life any resentment.' 'Though I am not clever,' replied Chung Kung, 'permit me to carry out these precepts.'

When Ssu-ma Niu asked for a definition of virtue, the Master said: 'The man of virtue is chary of speech.' 'He is chary of speech! Is this the meaning of virtue?' demanded Niu. 'When the doing of it is difficult,' responded Confucius, 'can one be other than chary of talking about it?'

When Ssu-ma Niu asked for a definition of the man of noble mind, the Master said: 'The man of noble mind has neither anxiety nor fear.'
'Neither anxiety nor fear!' he rejoined. 'Is this the definition of a noble man?'
'On searching within,' replied the Master, 'he finds no chronic ill, so why should he be anxious or why should he be afraid?'

Once when Ssu-ma Niu sorrowfully remarked, 'Other men all have their brothers, I alone am without,'[32] Tzu Hsia responded: 'I have heard it said, "Death and life are divine dispensations, and wealth and honours are with Heaven. When the man of noble

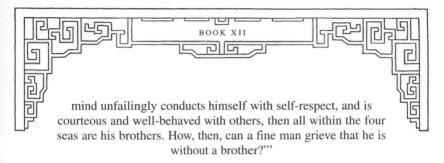

mind unfailingly conducts himself with self-respect, and is courteous and well-behaved with others, then all within the four seas are his brothers. How, then, can a fine man grieve that he is without a brother?"'

When Tzu Chang asked what was meant by insight, the Master replied: 'He who is unmoved by the insidious soaking in of slander, or by urgent representations of direct personal injury, may truly be called a man of insight. Indeed, he who is unmoved by the insidious soaking in of slander or by urgent representations of direct personal injury, may also indeed be called far-sighted.'

When Tzu Kung asked what were the essentials of government, the Master replied: 'Sufficient food, sufficient forces, and the confidence of the people.'
'Suppose,' rejoined Tzu Kung, 'I were compelled to dispense with one, which of these three should I forgo first?'
'Forgo the forces,' was the reply.
'Suppose,' said Tzu Kung, 'I were compelled to eliminate another, which of the other two should I forgo?'
'The food,' was the reply; 'for from of old death has been the lot of all men, but a people without faith cannot stand.'

Chi Tzu-Ch'eng[33] remarked: 'For a man of high character to be natural is quite sufficient; what need is there of art to make him such?'

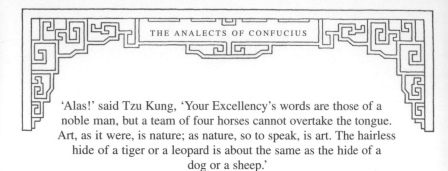
'Alas!' said Tzu Kung, 'Your Excellency's words are those of a noble man, but a team of four horses cannot overtake the tongue. Art, as it were, is nature; as nature, so to speak, is art. The hairless hide of a tiger or a leopard is about the same as the hide of a dog or a sheep.'

When Tzu Chang asked the best way to improve his character and to discriminate in what was irrational, the Master said: 'Take conscientiousness and sincerity as your ruling principles, submit also your mind to right conditions, and your character will improve. When you love a man you want him to live, when you hate him you wish he were dead; but you have already wanted him to live and yet again you wish he were dead. This is an instance of the irrational.
"Not indeed because of wealth,
But solely because talented."'

When Duke Ching of Ch'i inquired of Confucius the principles of government, Confucius answered saying: 'Let the prince be prince, the minister minister, the father father, and the son son.' 'Excellent!' said the Duke. 'Truly, if the prince be not prince, the minister not minister, the father not father, and the son not son, however much grain I may have, shall I be allowed to eat it?'

The Master said: 'Yu was a fellow! He could decide a dispute

with half a word.' Tzu Lu [Yu] never slept over a promise.

The Master said: 'I can try a lawsuit as well as other men, but surely the great thing is to bring about that there be no going to law.'

When Tzu Chang asked about the art of government, the Master replied: 'Ponder untiringly over your plans, and then conscientiously carry them into execution.'

The Master said: 'The man of noble mind seeks to achieve the good in others and not their evil. The little-minded man is the reverse of this.'

When Chi K'ang Tzu asked Confucius for a definition of government, Confucius replied: 'To govern means to guide aright. If you, Sir, will lead the way aright, who will dare to deviate from the right?'

Chi K'ang Tzu, being plagued with robbers, consulted Confucius, who answered him saying: 'If you, Sir, be free from

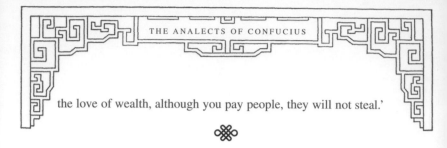

the love of wealth, although you pay people, they will not steal.'

Chi K'ang Tzu asked the opinion of Confucius on government and said: 'How would it do to execute the lawless for the good of the law-abiding?'

'What need, Sir, is there of capital punishment in your administration?' responded Confucius. 'If your aspirations are for good, Sir, the people will be good. The moral character of those in high position is the breeze, the character of those below is the grass. When the grass has the breeze upon it, it assuredly bends.'

Tzu Chang asked what a man must be like in order to gain general estimation.

'What is it that you mean by general estimation?' inquired the Master.

'To ensure popularity abroad and to ensure it at home,' replied Tzu Chang.

'That,' said the Master, 'is popularity, not esteem. As for the man who meets with general esteem, he is natural, upright, and a lover of justice; he weighs what men say and observes their expression, and his anxiety is to be more lowly than others; and so he ensures esteem abroad, as he ensures it also at home. As to the seeker of popularity, he assumes an air of magnanimity which his actions belie, while his self-assurance knows never a misgiving, and so he ensures popularity abroad, as he also ensures it at home.'

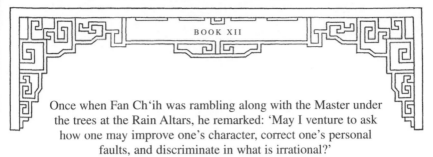

Once when Fan Ch'ih was rambling along with the Master under the trees at the Rain Altars, he remarked: 'May I venture to ask how one may improve one's character, correct one's personal faults, and discriminate in what is irrational?'

'An excellent question,' rejoined the Master. 'If a man put duty first and success after, will not that improve his character? If he attacks his own failings instead of those of others, will he not remedy his personal faults? For a morning's anger to forget his own safety and involve that of his relatives, is not this irrational?'

Once when Fan Ch'ih asked the meaning of virtue, the Master replied, 'Love your fellow men.'

On his asking the meaning of knowledge, the Master said: 'Know your fellow men.'

Fan Ch'ih not having comprehended, the Master added: 'By promoting the straight and degrading the crooked you can make even the crooked straight.'

Fan Ch'ih withdrew and afterwards meeting Tzu Hsia said to him: 'A little while ago, when I had an interview with the Master, and asked for a definition of knowledge, he replied, "By promoting the straight and degrading the crooked you can make even the crooked straight" – what can he have meant?'

'What a rich maxim that is!' replied Tzu Hsia. 'When Shun had the empire, he chose from amongst the multitude and promoted Kao Yao, whereupon all who were devoid of virtue disappeared. And when T'ang had the empire, he too chose from amongst the multitude and promoted I Yin, whereupon all who were devoid of virtue disappeared.'

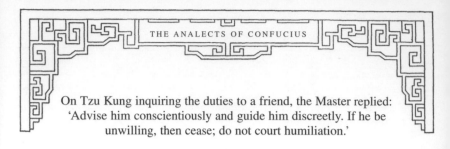

On Tzu Kung inquiring the duties to a friend, the Master replied: 'Advise him conscientiously and guide him discreetly. If he be unwilling, then cease; do not court humiliation.'

The philosopher Tseng said: 'The wise man by his culture gathers his friends, and by his friends develops his goodness of character.'

# BOOK XIII
## CHIEFLY CONCERNING GOVERNMENT

When Tzu Lu asked about the art of government the Master
replied: 'Be in advance of people; show them how to work.'
On his asking for something more, the Master added: 'Untiringly.'

When Chung Kung was minister for the House of Chi he asked
for advice on the art of government, whereupon the Master said:
'Utilize first and foremost your subordinate officers, overlook
their minor errors, and promote those who are worthy
and capable.'
'How may I know those who are worthy and capable?' he asked.
'Promote those you do recognize;' was the reply; 'as to those

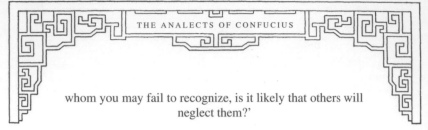

whom you may fail to recognize, is it likely that others will
neglect them?'

'The Prince of Wei,' said Tzu Lu, 'is awaiting you, Sir, to take
control of his administration – what will you undertake first, Sir?'
'The one thing needed,' replied the Master, 'is the correction
of terms.'
'Are you as wide of the mark as that, Sir?' said Tzu Lu. 'Why
this correcting?'
'How uncultivated you are, Yu!' responded the Master. 'A wise man,
in regard to what he does not understand, maintains an attitude of
reserve. If terms be incorrect, then statements do not accord with
facts; and when statements and facts do not accord, then business is
not properly executed; when business is not properly executed, order
and harmony do not flourish; when order and harmony do not
flourish, then justice becomes arbitrary; and when justice becomes
arbitrary, the people do not know how to move hand or foot. Hence
whatever a wise man states he can always define, and what he so
defines, he can always carry into practice; for the wise man will on
no account have anything remiss in his definitions.'

On Fan Ch'ih requesting to be taught agriculture, the Master
replied, 'I am not as good as an old farmer for that.' When he asked
to be taught gardening the Master answered, 'I am not as good as
an old gardener for that.' On Fan Ch'ih withdrawing, the Master
said: 'What a little-minded man is Fan Hsü! When a ruler loves
good manners, his people will not let themselves be disrespectful;

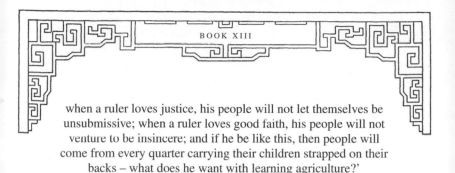

when a ruler loves justice, his people will not let themselves be
unsubmissive; when a ruler loves good faith, his people will not
venture to be insincere; and if he be like this, then people will
come from every quarter carrying their children strapped on their
backs – what does he want with learning agriculture?'

The Master said: 'A man may be able to recite the three hundred
Odes, but if, when given a post in the administration, he proves to
be without practical ability, or when sent anywhere on a mission,
he is unable of himself to answer a question, although his
knowledge is extensive, of what use is it?'

The Master said: 'If a ruler is himself upright, his people will do
their duty without orders; but if he himself be not upright,
although he may order they will not obey.'

The Master said of [Prince] Ching, a scion of the ducal House of
Wei, that he dwelt well content in his house. When first he began
to possess property, he called it 'a passable accumulation'; when
he had prospered somewhat, he called it 'passably complete'; and
when he had amassed plenty, he called it 'passably fine'.

When the Master was travelling to Wei, Jan Yu drove him. 'What a
numerous population!' remarked the Master.

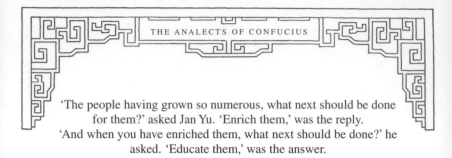

'The people having grown so numerous, what next should be done for them?' asked Jan Yu. 'Enrich them,' was the reply. 'And when you have enriched them, what next should be done?' he asked. 'Educate them,' was the answer.

The Master said: 'Were any prince to employ me, in a twelvemonth something could have been done, but in three years the work could be completed.'

The Master remarked: 'How true is the saying: "If good men ruled the country for a hundred years, they could even tame the brutal and abolish capital punishment!"'

The Master said: 'If a kingly ruler were to arise, it would take a generation before virtue prevailed, however.'

The Master said: 'If a man put himself aright, what difficulty will he have in the public service; but if he cannot put himself aright, how is he going to put others right?'

Duke Ting [of Lu] inquired whether there were any one phrase by the adoption of which a country could be made prosperous.

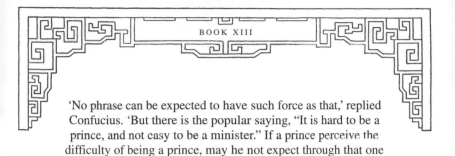
'No phrase can be expected to have such force as that,' replied
Confucius. 'But there is the popular saying, "It is hard to be a
prince, and not easy to be a minister." If a prince perceive the
difficulty of being a prince, may he not expect through that one
phrase to prosper his country?'

'Is there any one phrase,' he asked, 'through which a country may
be ruined?'

'No phrase can be expected to have such force as that,' replied
Confucius. 'But there is the popular saying, "I should have no
gratification in being a prince, unless none opposed my
commands." If those are good, and no one opposes them, that
surely is well. But if they are not good, and no one opposes them,
may he not expect in that one phrase to ruin his country?'

When the Duke of She[34] asked the meaning of good government,
the Master answered: 'The near are happy and the distant
attracted.'

When Tzu Hsia was magistrate of Chü-fu,[35] he asked what should
be his policy, whereupon the Master said: 'Do not be in a hurry; do
not be intent on minor advantages. When one is in a hurry, nothing
is thorough; and when one is intent on minor advantages, nothing
great is accomplished.'

Once when Fan Ch'ih asked about virtue, the Master said: 'In
private life be courteous, in handling public business be serious,

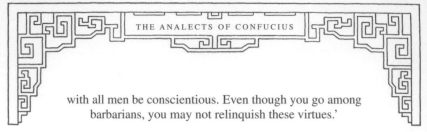
with all men be conscientious. Even though you go among barbarians, you may not relinquish these virtues.'

Tzu Kung asked: 'What must an official be like to merit his name?' 'If in his personal conduct,' replied the Master, 'he has a sensibility to dishonour, and wheresoever he be sent will not disgrace his prince's commission, he may be said to merit his title.' 'I would venture to ask who may be ranked lower,' said Tzu Kung. 'He whom his relatives commend as filial and whose neighbours commend as brotherly,' was the answer. 'I venture to ask the next lower,' said Tzu Kung. 'He is one who always stands by his word,' was the answer, 'and who persists in all he undertakes; he is a man of grit, though of narrow outlook; yet perhaps he may be taken as of the third class.' 'What would you say of the present-day government officials?' asked Tzu Kung. 'Faugh!' said the Master. 'A set of pecks and hampers, unworthy to be taken into account!'

The Master said: 'If I cannot obtain men of the Golden Mean to teach, those whom I must have, let them be the ambitious and the discreet; for the ambitious do make progress and take hold, and as to the discreet, there are things that they will refuse to sanction.'

The Master said: 'The true gentleman is friendly but not familiar; the inferior man is familiar but not friendly.' Tzu Kung asked: 'What would you say of the man who is liked by all his fellow townsmen?' 'That is not sufficient,' was the reply. 'Then what

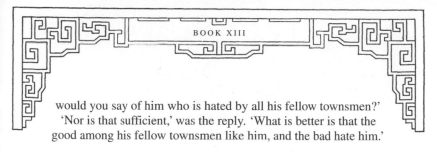
would you say of him who is hated by all his fellow townsmen?'
'Nor is that sufficient,' was the reply. 'What is better is that the
good among his fellow townsmen like him, and the bad hate him.'

The Master said: 'The true gentleman is easy to serve, yet difficult
to please. If you attempt to please him in any improper way, he
will be displeased; but when it comes to appointing men in their
work, he has regard to their capacity. The inferior man is hard to
serve, yet easy to please. If you attempt to please him, even in an
improper way, he will be pleased; but in appointing men their
work, he expects them to be fit for everything.'

The Master said: 'The well-bred are dignified but not pompous.
The ill-bred are pompous, but not dignified.'

The Master said: 'The firm of spirit, the resolute in character, the
simple in manner, and the slow of speech are not far from virtue.'

Tzu Lu asked: 'What qualities must one possess to be entitled to
be called an educated man?' 'He who is earnest in spirit,
persuasive in speech, and withal of gracious bearing,' said the
Master, 'may be called an educated man – earnest in spirit
and persuasive of speech with his friends, and of gracious
bearing towards his brothers.'

# BOOK XIV
## CHIEFLY CONCERNING GOVERNMENT AND CERTAIN RULERS

When Hsien[36] asked the meaning of dishonour, the Master said:
'When his country is well-governed to be thinking only of pay,
and when his country is ill-governed to be thinking only of pay –
that is dishonour for a man.'

Hsien again asked: 'If a man refrains from ambition, boasting,
resentment, and selfish desire, it may, I suppose, be counted
to him for virtue.' 'It may be counted for difficult,' said the
Master, 'but whether that alone is virtue, I know not.'

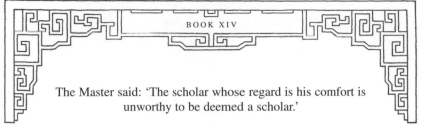

The Master said: 'The scholar whose regard is his comfort is unworthy to be deemed a scholar.'

The Master said: 'When law and order prevail in the land, a man may be bold in speech and bold in action; but when the land lacks law and order, though he may take bold action, he should lay restraint on his speech.'

The Master said: 'A man of principle is sure to have something good to say, but he who has something good to say is not necessarily a man of principle. A virtuous man is sure to be courageous, but a courageous man is not necessarily a man of virtue.'

Nan Kung Kua remarked to Confucius by way of inquiry: 'Is it not a fact that Prince I excelled as an archer, and Ao could propel a boat on dry land, yet neither died a natural death, while Yü and Chi, who took a personal interest in agriculture, became possessed of the empire?'[37]

The Master made no reply, but when Nan Kung Kua had withdrawn, he observed: 'A scholar indeed is such a man! Such a man has a true estimation of virtue!'

'There may perhaps be men of the higher type who fail in virtue,

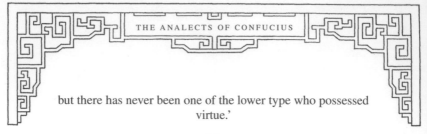
but there has never been one of the lower type who possessed virtue.'

The Master said: 'Can love be other than exacting, or loyalty refrain from admonition?'

The Master said: 'To be poor and not complain is difficult; to be rich and not arrogant is easy.'

When Tzu Lu asked what constituted the character of the perfect man, the Master replied: 'If he have the sagacity of Tsang Wu Chung, the purity of Kung Ch'o, the courage of Chuang Tzu of P'ien, and the skill of Jan Ch'iu,[38] and if he refines these with the arts of courtesy and harmony, then, indeed, he may be deemed a perfect man.'

'But what need is there,' he added, 'for the perfect man of the present day to be like this? Let him when he sees anything to his advantage think whether it be right; when he meets with danger be ready to lay down his life; and, however long-standing the undertaking, let him not belie the professions of his whole life: then he, too, may be deemed a perfect man.'

The Master put a question to Kung-ming Chia about Kung-shu Wen-tzu,[39] and said: 'Is it really true that your Master neither

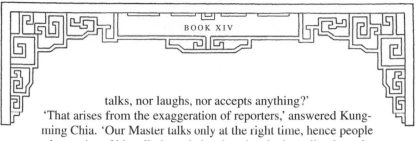

talks, nor laughs, nor accepts anything?'
'That arises from the exaggeration of reporters,' answered Kung-ming Chia. 'Our Master talks only at the right time, hence people do not tire of his talk; he only laughs when he is really pleased, hence people do not tire of his laughter; he only accepts things when it is right to do so, hence men do not tire of his accepting.'
'Is that so?' said the Master. 'Can that indeed be so?'

The Minister Chüan, formerly a retainer of Kung-shu Wen-tzu, afterwards went up to court in company with Wen-tzu. The Master on hearing of it observed: 'Wen well deserves to be considered "a promoter of culture".'

When the Master was speaking of the unprincipled character of Duke Ling of Wei,[40] K'ang-tzu observed: 'Such being the case, how is it he does not lose his throne?'
'Chung-shu Yü,' answered Confucius, 'has charge of the envoys; the Reader T'o has charge of the ancestral temple; Wang-sun Chia commands the forces – and, such being the case, how should he lose his throne?'

The Master said: 'He who speaks without modesty will perform with difficulty.'

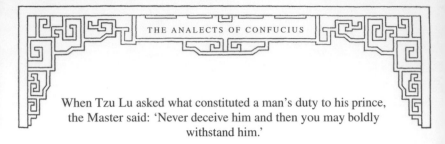
When Tzu Lu asked what constituted a man's duty to his prince, the Master said: 'Never deceive him and then you may boldly withstand him.'

The Master said: 'The progress of the nobler-minded man is upwards, the progress of the inferior man is downwards.'

The Master said: 'The men of old studied for the sake of self-improvement; the men of the present day study for the approbation of others.'

Chü Po Yü[41] having sent a messenger to convey his respects to Confucius, Confucius made him sit down along with him and questioned him, asking: 'What is your master doing now?' The messenger replied: 'My master is seeking to make his faults fewer, but has not yet succeeded.'
When the messenger had withdrawn, the Master observed: 'What a messenger! What a messenger!'

The Master said: 'He who does not occupy the office does not discuss its policy.'

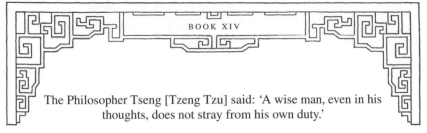

The Philosopher Tseng [Tzeng Tzu] said: 'A wise man, even in his thoughts, does not stray from his own duty.'

The Master said: 'The higher type of man is modest in what he says, but surpasses in what he does.'

The Master said: 'There are three characteristics of the noble man's life, to which I cannot lay claim: being virtuous he is free from care; possessing knowledge he is free from doubts; being courageous he is free from fear.'
'That is what you say of yourself!' replied Tzu Kung.

Tzu Kung being in the habit of making comparisons, the Master observed: 'How worthy Tzu must be! As for me, I have not the time to spare.'

The Master said: 'A wise man is not distressed that people do not know him; he is distressed at his own lack of ability.'

The Master said: 'Is not he a man of real worth who does not anticipate deceit nor imagine that people will doubt his word;

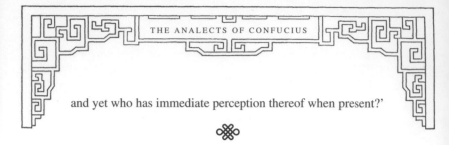

and yet who has immediate perception thereof when present?'

Wei-sheng Mou,[42] sneering at Confucius, said: 'Ch'iu, what are you doing with this "perching here and perching there"? Are you not making a business of talking to please people?'
'I should not dare to talk only to please people,' replied Confucius; 'and I should hate to be obstinately immovable.'

The Master said: 'A good horse is not praised for its strength but for its character.'

Some one asked: 'What do you think about the principle of rewarding enmity with kindness?'
'With what, then, would you reward kindness?' asked the Master.
'Reward enmity with just treatment, and kindness with kindness.'

'No one knows me, alas!' exclaimed the Master. 'Why do you say, Master, that no one knows you?' said Tzu Kung. 'I make no complaint against Heaven,' replied the Master, 'nor blame men, for though my studies are lowly, my mind soars aloft; and does not Heaven know me?'

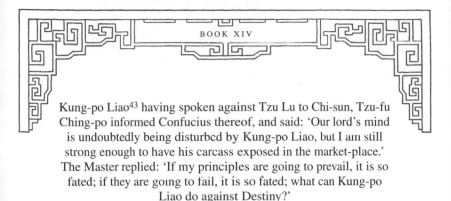

Kung-po Liao[43] having spoken against Tzu Lu to Chi-sun, Tzu-fu Ching-po informed Confucius thereof, and said: 'Our lord's mind is undoubtedly being disturbed by Kung-po Liao, but I am still strong enough to have his carcass exposed in the market-place.' The Master replied: 'If my principles are going to prevail, it is so fated; if they are going to fail, it is so fated; what can Kung-po Liao do against Destiny?'

The Master said: 'Some good men withdraw from the world. Withdrawal from fatherland comes next in order; next is from uncongenial looks; and next is from uncongenial language.'

The Master said: 'There are seven men who have done this.'

On one occasion when Tzu Lu happened to spend the night at Stone Gate, the gate opener asked him, 'Where are you from?' 'Master K'ung's,' replied Tzu Lu.
'Is not he the one who knows he cannot succeed and keeps on trying to do so?' was the response.

Tzu Chang said: 'The *Book of History* says that when Kao Tsung[44] observed the imperial mourning he did not speak for three years. What may be the meaning of that?'
'Why need you specialize Kao Tsung? All the men of old did the

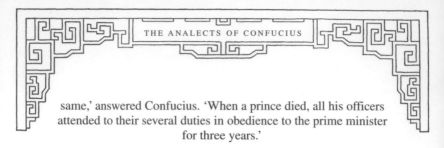

same,' answered Confucius. 'When a prince died, all his officers attended to their several duties in obedience to the prime minister for three years.'

The Master said: 'When those in high position are fond of orderly behaviour, service from the people is easily commanded.'

When Tzu Lu asked what should be the character of a man of the nobler order, the Master replied: 'He should cultivate himself unfailingly to respect others.'
'Will it suffice to be like this?' asked Tzu Lu.
'He should cultivate himself so as to ease the lot of others,' was the reply.
'And is this sufficient?' asked Tzu Lu.
'He should cultivate himself so as to ease the lot of the people. He should cultivate himself so as to ease the lot of the people – even Yao and Shun[45] ever remained assiduous about this!'

Yüan Jang[46] sat squatting and waiting as the Master approached, who said to him: 'When young being mannerless, when grown up doing nothing worthy of mention, when old not dying – this is being a rogue!' And with this he hit him on the shank with his staff.

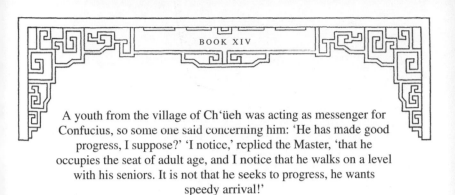

A youth from the village of Ch'üeh was acting as messenger for Confucius, so some one said concerning him: 'He has made good progress, I suppose?' 'I notice,' replied the Master, 'that he occupies the seat of adult age, and I notice that he walks on a level with his seniors. It is not that he seeks to progress, he wants speedy arrival!'

# BOOK XV
## CHIEFLY ON THE MAINTENANCE OF PRINCIPLES AND
## CHARACTER

When Duke Ling of Wei[40] asked Confucius about military tactics,
Confucius replied: 'With the appurtenances of worship I have
indeed an acquaintance, but as to military matters I have never
studied them.' Next day he straightway took his departure.
On the way in Ch'en their supplies failed, and his followers were
so ill that they could not stand. Tzu Lu with some irritation
sought an interview and said: 'Does a man of the higher order
also have to suffer want?' 'The superior man bears want
unshaken,' replied the Master, 'the inferior man in want
becomes demoralized.'

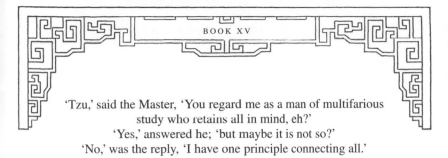

'Tzu,' said the Master, 'You regard me as a man of multifarious study who retains all in mind, eh?'
'Yes,' answered he; 'but maybe it is not so?'
'No,' was the reply, 'I have one principle connecting all.'

'Yu,' said the Master, 'there are few who understand virtue.'

The Master said: 'May not Shun[45] be instanced as one who made no effort, yet the empire was well governed? For what effort did he make? Ordering himself in all seriousness, he did nothing but maintain the correct imperial attitude.'

When Tzu Chang asked how to succeed with others, the Master made answer: 'If you are sincere and truthful in what you say, and trustworthy and circumspect in what you do, then although you be in the land of the barbarians you will succeed with them. But if you are not sincere and truthful in what you say, and untrustworthy and not circumspect in what you do, are you likely to succeed even in your own country? When standing, see these principles there in front of you. When in your carriage, see them resting on the yoke. Then you will succeed everywhere.'
Tzu Chang inscribed these counsels on his sash.

The Master said: 'What a straight man was the recorder Yü![47]

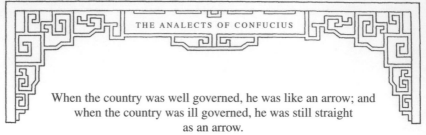

When the country was well governed, he was like an arrow; and
when the country was ill governed, he was still straight
as an arrow.

'What a noble man is Chü Po Yü! When the country is well
governed, he holds office; but when the country is ill governed, he
. can roll up his portfolio and keep it in his bosom.'

'Not to enlighten one who can be enlightened is to waste a man;
to enlighten one who cannot be enlightened is to waste words. The
intelligent man neither wastes his man nor his words.'

The Master said: 'The resolute scholar and the virtuous man will
not seek life at the expense of virtue. Some even sacrifice their
lives to crown their virtue.'

When Tzu Kung asked about the practice of virtue, the Master
replied: 'A workman who wants to do his work well must first
sharpen his tools. In whatever state you dwell, take service with
the worthiest of its ministers, and make friends of the most
virtuous of its scholars.'

Yen Yüan once asked about the administration of a state.
The Master replied: 'Adopt the calendar of Hsia; ride in the state

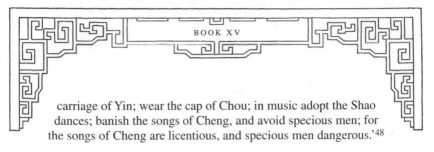
carriage of Yin; wear the cap of Chou; in music adopt the Shao dances; banish the songs of Cheng, and avoid specious men; for the songs of Cheng are licentious, and specious men dangerous.'[48]

The Master said: 'Who heeds not the future will find sorrow at hand.'

'It is all in vain!' said the Master. 'I have never yet seen a man as fond of virtue as of [female] beauty.'

The Master said: 'He who demands much from himself and little from others will avoid resentment.'

The Master said: 'If a man does not ask himself, "What am I to make of this?" "What am I to make of that?" – there is nothing whatever I can make of him.'

The Master said: 'Men who associate together the livelong day and whose conversation never rises to what is just and right, but whose delight is in deeds of petty shrewdness – how hard is their case!'

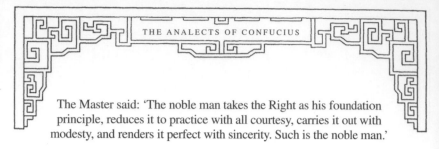

The Master said: 'The noble man takes the Right as his foundation principle, reduces it to practice with all courtesy, carries it out with modesty, and renders it perfect with sincerity. Such is the noble man.'

The Master remarked: 'The noble man is pained over his own incompetency; he is not pained that others ignore him.'

The Master said: 'The noble man seeks what he wants in himself; the inferior man seeks it from others.'

The Master said: 'The noble man upholds his dignity without striving for it; he is sociable without entering any clique.'

The Master said: 'The wise man does not appreciate a man because of what he says; nor does he depreciate what he says because of the man.'

'Is there any one word,' asked Tzu Kung, 'which could be adopted as a lifelong rule of conduct?' The Master replied: 'Is not Sympathy the word? Do not do to others what you would not like yourself.'

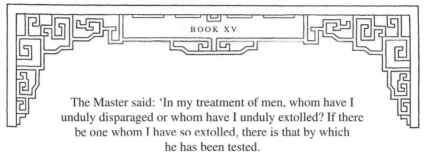

The Master said: 'In my treatment of men, whom have I unduly disparaged or whom have I unduly extolled? If there be one whom I have so extolled, there is that by which he has been tested.

'Thus and with such people the Three Dynasties pursued their straightforward course.'

The Master said: 'I can still go back to the days when a recorder left a temporary blank in his records, and when a man who had a horse would lend it to another to ride. Now, alas! such a condition no more exists.'

The Master said: 'Plausible words confound morals, and a trifling impatience may confound a great project.'

The Master said: 'Though all hate a man, one must investigate the cause; and though all like him, one must also investigate the cause.'

The Master said: 'A man can enlarge his principles; it is not his principles that enlarge the man.'

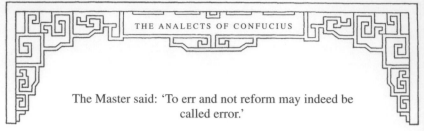

The Master said: 'To err and not reform may indeed be called error.'

The Master said: 'I have spent the whole day without food and the whole night without sleep in order to think. It was of no use. It is better to learn.'

The Master said: 'The wise man makes duty, not a living, his aim; for there is hunger even for a farmer, and sometimes emolument for a scholar! But the wise man is anxious about his duty, not about poverty.'

The Master said: 'If a man intellectually realizes a given principle, but if his moral character does not enable him to live up to it, even though he has reached it, he will decline from it. Though intellectually he has attained to it, and his moral character enables him to live up to it, if he does not govern people with dignity, they will not respect him. And though he has intellectually attained to it, his moral character enables him to live up to it, and he governs with dignity, if he instigates the people to act in a disorderly manner, he is still lacking in excellence.'

The Master said: 'A man of the higher type may not be

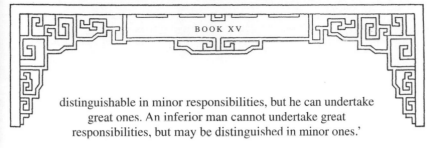

distinguishable in minor responsibilities, but he can undertake great ones. An inferior man cannot undertake great responsibilities, but may be distinguished in minor ones.'

The Master said: 'Virtue is more to man than either water or fire. I have seen men die through walking into water or fire, but I have never seen a man die through walking the path of virtue.'

The Master said: 'He upon whom a moral duty devolves should not give way even to his master.'

The Master said: 'The wise man is intelligently, not blindly, loyal.'

The Master said: 'In serving one's prince, one should give careful attention to his business, and make the pay a secondary consideration.'

The Master said: 'In teaching there should be no class distinctions.'

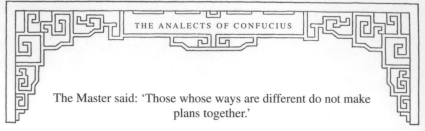

The Master said: 'Those whose ways are different do not make plans together.'

The Master said: 'In language perspicuity is everything.'

The State Bandmaster Mien[49] once called to see him. On arriving at the steps the Master said, 'Here are the steps.' On coming to the mat, he said, 'Here is your mat.' When all were seated the Master informed him: 'So and so is here, so and so is there.'
When the Bandmaster had gone, Tzu Chang inquired: 'Is it the proper thing to tell a Bandmaster those things?' 'Yes,' answered the Master, 'undoubtedly it is the proper thing for a blind Bandmaster's guide to do so.'

# BOOK XVI
### CONCERNING MINISTERIAL RESPONSIBILITY ET ALIA

The chief of the House of Chi being about to invade the minor
principality of Chuan-yü, Jan Yu and Chi Lu interviewed Confucius
and said: 'Our chief is about to commence operations against Chuan-
yü fief.' 'Ch'iu,' said Confucius, 'is not this misdeed yours? The
Head of Chuan-yü was appointed by the ancient kings to preside
over the sacrifices to the Eastern Meng; the fief also is within the
boundaries of our state, and its ruler is direct sacrificial minister of
the crown. What business has your chief with attacking it?'
'It is our master's wish,' said Jan Yu, 'neither of us two ministers
wishes it.' 'Ch'iu,' replied Confucius, 'Chou Jen had a saying: "Let
him who is allowed to use his ability retain his position, and let
him who cannot retire. Of what use is he as a blind man's guide,
who neither holds him up when tottering, nor supports him when

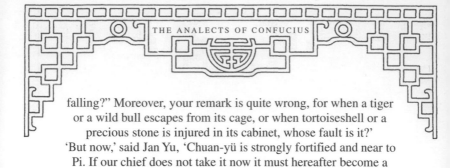

falling?" Moreover, your remark is quite wrong, for when a tiger or a wild bull escapes from its cage, or when tortoiseshell or a precious stone is injured in its cabinet, whose fault is it?'

'But now,' said Jan Yu, 'Chuan-yü is strongly fortified and near to Pi. If our chief does not take it now it must hereafter become a cause of anxiety to his descendants.'

'Ch'iu,' replied Confucius, 'the man of honour detests those who decline to say plainly that they want a thing and insist on making excuses in regard thereto. I have heard that the ruler of a kingdom, or the chief of a house, is not concerned about his people being few, but about lack of equitable treatment; nor is he concerned over poverty, but over the presence of discontent; for where there is equity there is no poverty, where concord prevails there is no lack of people, and where contentment reigns there are no upheavals. Such a state of things existing, then, if any outlying people are still unsubmissive he attracts them by the promotion of culture and morality, and when he has attracted them he makes them contented. But here are you two, Yu and Ch'iu, assisting your chief; for though an outlying people are unsubmissive, he cannot attract them; and though the state is disorganized and disrupted, he cannot preserve it. And yet he is planning to take up arms within his own state. I myself fear that Chi-sun's cause for anxiety does not lie in Chuan-yü, but within his own gate-screen [his palace]!'

Confucius said: 'When good government prevails in the empire, civil ordinances and punitive expeditions issue from the emperor. When good government fails in the empire, civil ordinance and punitive expeditions issue from the nobles. When they issue from a noble, it is rare if the empire be not lost within ten generations. When they issue from a noble's minister, it is rare if the empire be

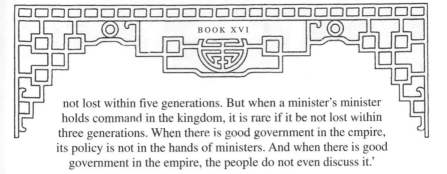

not lost within five generations. But when a minister's minister holds command in the kingdom, it is rare if it be not lost within three generations. When there is good government in the empire, its policy is not in the hands of ministers. And when there is good government in the empire, the people do not even discuss it.'

Confucius said: 'There are three kinds of friends that are beneficial, and three that are harmful. To make friends with the upright, with the faithful, with the well-informed, is beneficial. To make friends with the plausible, with the insinuating, with the glib, is harmful.'

Confucius said: 'There are three ways of pleasure-seeking that are beneficial, and there are three that are harmful. To seek pleasure in the refinements of manners and music, to seek pleasure in discussing the excellences of others, to seek pleasure in making many worthy friends – these are beneficial. To seek pleasure in unbridled enjoyment, to seek pleasure in looseness and gadding, to seek pleasure in conviviality – these are harmful.'

Confucius said: 'There are three errors to be avoided when in the presence of a superior: to speak before being called upon, which may be termed forwardness; not to speak when called upon, which may be termed timidity; and to speak before noting a superior's expression, which may be called blindness.'

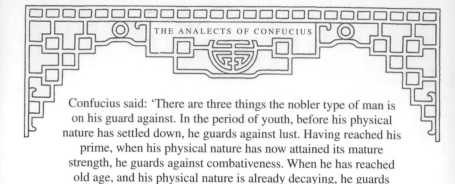

Confucius said: 'There are three things the nobler type of man is on his guard against. In the period of youth, before his physical nature has settled down, he guards against lust. Having reached his prime, when his physical nature has now attained its mature strength, he guards against combativeness. When he has reached old age, and his physical nature is already decaying, he guards against acquisitiveness.'

Confucius said: 'The man of noble mind holds three things in awe. He holds the Divine Will in awe; he holds the great in awe; and he holds the precepts of the sages in awe. The baser man, not knowing the Divine Will, does not stand in awe of it; he takes liberties with the great; and makes a mock of the precepts of the sages.'

Confucius said: 'Those who have innate wisdom take highest rank. Those who acquire it by study rank next. Those who learn despite natural limitations come next. But those who are of limited ability and yet will not learn – these form the lowest class of men.'

Confucius said: 'The wise man has nine points of thoughtful care. In looking, his care is to observe distinctly; in listening, his care is to apprehend clearly; in his appearance, his care is to be kindly; in his manner, his care is to be courteous; in speaking, his care is to be conscientious; in his duties, his care is to be earnest; in doubt, his care is to seek information; in anger, he has a care for the

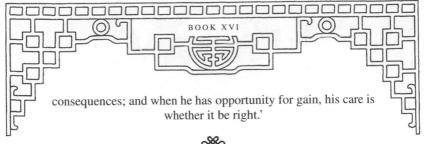

consequences; and when he has opportunity for gain, his care is
whether it be right.'

Confucius said: '"They look up at the good as if fearing not to
reach it, and shrink from evil as if from scalding water." I have
seen such men, as I have heard such sayings. "They dwell in
seclusion to think out their aims, and practise right living in order
to extend their principles" – I have heard such sayings, but I have
never seen such men.'

Ch'en K'ang once asked Po Yü: 'Have you ever had any lesson
different from the rest of us from the Master?'
'No,' was the reply, 'but he was once standing alone, and as I
hastened across the hall, he remarked: "Have you studied the
Odes?" "No," I replied. "If you do not study the Odes," he said,
"you will have nothing to use in conversation." On going out I set
myself to study the Odes.
'Another day, he was again standing alone, and as I hastened
across the hall, he asked: "Have you studied the Rules of
Ceremony?" "No," I replied, "If you do not study the Ceremonies,
you will have no grounding." On going out I set myself to study
the Ceremonies. These are the two lessons I have received.'
When Ch'en K'ang came away he remarked with delight, 'I asked
one thing and obtained three – I have learnt about the Odes, I have
learnt about the Ceremonies, and I have learnt that the Wise Man
keeps his son at a distance.'

## BOOK XVII
### RECORDING UNSUITABLE CALLS AND SUNDRY MAXIMS

The Master said: 'By nature men nearly resemble each other; in practice they grow wide apart.'

The Master said: 'It is only the very wisest and the very stupidest who never change.'

When the Master arrived at Wu city, he heard everywhere the sound of stringed instruments and singing; whereupon he smiled and laughingly said, 'Why use a cleaver to kill a chicken?'

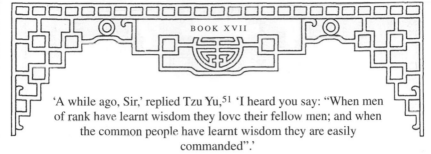

'A while ago, Sir,' replied Tzu Yu,[51] 'I heard you say: "When men of rank have learnt wisdom they love their fellow men; and when the common people have learnt wisdom they are easily commanded".'

'My disciples!' said the Master, 'Yen's remark is right. What I said before was only in jest.'

Tzu Chang asked Confucius the meaning of virtue, to which Confucius replied: 'To be able everywhere one goes to carry five things into practice constitutes Virtue.' On begging to know what they were, he was told: 'They are courtesy, magnanimity, sincerity, earnestness, and kindness. With courtesy you will avoid insult, with magnanimity you will win all, with sincerity men will trust you, with earnestness you will have success, and with kindness you will be well fitted to command others.'

Pi Hsi[52] sent a formal invitation and the Master was inclined to go. But Tzu Lu observed: 'Once upon a time, I heard you say, Sir, "With the man who is personally engaged in a wrongful enterprise, the man of honour declines to associate." Pi Hsi is holding Chung-mou in revolt, what will it be like, Sir, if you go there?'

'True,' said the Master, 'I did use those words; but is it not said of the really hard, that you may grind it and it will not grind down; also is it not said of the really white, that you may dye it but it will not turn black? Am I indeed a bitter gourd? Must I, like it, be hung up and never eaten?'

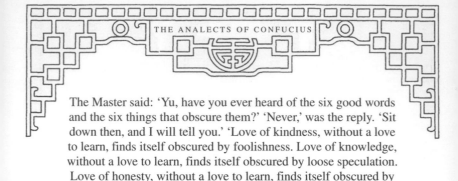

The Master said: 'Yu, have you ever heard of the six good words and the six things that obscure them?' 'Never,' was the reply. 'Sit down then, and I will tell you.' 'Love of kindness, without a love to learn, finds itself obscured by foolishness. Love of knowledge, without a love to learn, finds itself obscured by loose speculation. Love of honesty, without a love to learn, finds itself obscured by harmful candour. Love of straightforwardness, without a love to learn, finds itself obscured by misdirected judgement. Love of daring, without a love to learn, finds itself obscured by insubordination. And love for strength of character, without a love to learn, finds itself obscured by intractability.'

The Master said: 'My sons, my disciples, why do you not study the poets? Poetry is able to stimulate the mind, it can train to observation, it can encourage social intercourse, it can modify the vexations of life; from it the student learns to fulfil his more immediate duty to his parents, and his remoter duty to his prince; and in it he may become widely acquainted with the names of birds and beasts, plants and trees.'

The Master said to his son Po Yü: 'Have you studied the Chou Nan and the Chao Nan?[53] Is not the man who does not study the Chou Nan and the Chao Nan Odes like one who stands with his face hard up against a wall, eh?'

The Master said: 'He who shams a stern appearance while

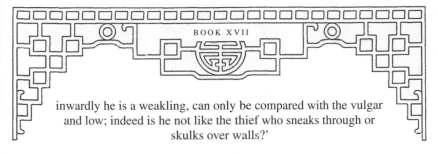

inwardly he is a weakling, can only be compared with the vulgar and low; indeed is he not like the thief who sneaks through or skulks over walls?'

The Master said: 'To proclaim on the road what you hear on the way is virtue thrown away.'

'These servile fellows!' said the Master. 'How is it possible to serve one's prince along with them? Before obtaining their position they are in anxiety to obtain it, and when they have it they are in anxiety lest they lose it; and if men are in anxiety about losing their position, there is no length to which they will not go.'

'In olden times,' said the Master, 'the people had three faults, which nowadays perhaps no longer exist. High spirit in olden times meant liberty in detail; the high spirit of today means utter looseness. Dignity of old meant reserve; dignity today means resentment and offence. Simple-mindedness of old meant straightforwardness; simple-mindedness today is nothing but a mask for cunning.'

The Master said: 'Artful address and an insinuating demeanour seldom accompany virtue.'

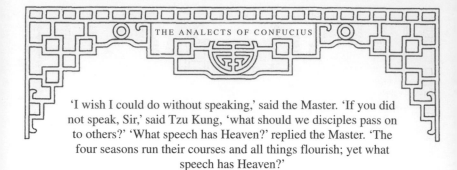
'I wish I could do without speaking,' said the Master. 'If you did not speak, Sir,' said Tzu Kung, 'what should we disciples pass on to others?' 'What speech has Heaven?' replied the Master. 'The four seasons run their courses and all things flourish; yet what speech has Heaven?'

Ju Pei[54] wished to see Confucius, who excused himself on the grounds of sickness; but when the messenger had gone out at the door, he took up his harpsichord and began to sing, so that Ju Pei might hear it.

Tsai Wo, asking about the three years' mourning, suggested that one year was long enough. 'If,' said he, 'a well-bred man be three years without exercising his manners, his manners will certainly degenerate; and if for three years he make no use of music, his music will certainly go to ruin. In one year the last year's grain is finished and the new grain has been garnered, the seasonal friction-sticks have made their varying fires – a year would be enough.' 'Would you, then, feel at ease in eating good rice and wearing fine clothes?' asked the Master.

'I should,' was the reply.

'If you would feel at ease, then do so; but a well-bred man, when mourning, does not relish good food when he eats it, does not enjoy music when he hears it, and does not feel at ease when in a comfortable dwelling; therefore he avoids those things. But now you would feel at ease, so go and do them.'

When Tsai had gone out, the Master said: 'The unfeelingness of

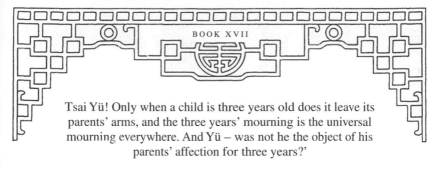

Tsai Yü! Only when a child is three years old does it leave its parents' arms, and the three years' mourning is the universal mourning everywhere. And Yü – was not he the object of his parents' affection for three years?'

The Master said: 'How hard is the case of the man who stuffs himself with food the livelong day, never applying his mind to anything! Are there no checkers or chess to play? Even to do that is surely better than nothing at all.'

Tzu Lu once asked: 'Does a man of the nobler class hold courage in estimation?'
'Men of the nobler class,' said the Master, 'deem rectitude the highest thing. It is men of the nobler class, with courage but without rectitude, who rebel. It is men of the lower order, with courage but without rectitude, who become robbers.'

'Do men of the nobler class detest others?' asked Tzu Kung.
'They do detest others,' answered the Master. 'They detest men who divulge other people's misdeeds. They detest those low, base people who slander their superiors. They detest the bold and mannerless. They detest the persistently forward who are yet obtuse. And have you, Tzu, those whom you detest?' he asked.
'I detest those who count prying out information as wisdom. I detest those who count absence of modesty as courage. I detest

those who count denouncing a man's private affairs as straightforwardness,' replied Tzu Kung.

The Master said: 'Of all people, maids and servants are hardest to keep in your house. If you are friendly with them they lose their deference; if you are reserved with them they resent it.'

The Master said: 'If a man reach forty and yet be disliked by his fellows, he will be so to the end.'

# BOOK XVIII
## CONCERNING ANCIENT WORTHIES

The viscount of Wei withdrew from serving the tyrant Chou;[55] the viscount of Chi was made a slave; Pi Kan remonstrated with the tyrant and suffered death. The Master said: 'The Yin Dynasty thus had three men of virtue.'

Hui of Liu-hsia[56] filled the office of Chief Criminal Judge, but had been repeatedly dismissed, and people said to him, 'Is it not time, sir, for you to be going elsewhere?'
'If I do honest public service,' said he, 'where shall I go and not be often dismissed? And if I am willing to do dishonest public

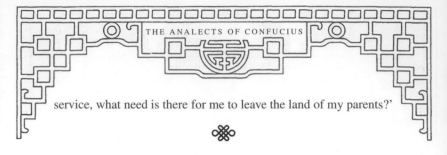

service, what need is there for me to leave the land of my parents?'

Ch'ang Chü and Chieh Ni[57] were cultivating their land together
when Confucius was passing that way, so he sent Tzu Lu to
inquire for the ford.
'And who is that holding the reins in the carriage?' asked Ch'ang
Chü. 'It is Kung Ch'iu,' replied Tzu Lu. 'Is it Kung Ch'iu of Lu
[Confucius]?' he asked. 'It is,' was the reply. 'Then he knows the
ford,' said he.
Tzu Lu then questioned Chieh Ni. 'Who are you, sir?' asked Chieh
Ni. 'I am Chung Yu,' was the answer. 'Are you a disciple of Kung
Ch'iu of Lu?' 'Yes,' replied he. 'All the world is rushing headlong
like a swelling torrent and who will help you to remedy it?' he
asked. 'As for you, instead of following a leader who flees from
one after another, had you not better follow those who flee the
world entirely?' With this he fell to raking in his seed without
a pause.
Tzu Lu went off and reported to his Master what they said, who
remarked with surprise: 'I cannot herd with birds and beasts; if I
may not associate with mankind, with whom then am I to
associate? Did right rule prevail in the world, I should not be
taking part in reforming it.'

Once when Tzu Lu was following the Master on a journey he
happened to fall behind. Meeting an old man carrying a basket on
his staff, Tzu Lu asked him, 'Have you seen my Master, sir?'
'You,' said the old man, 'whose four limbs know not toil, and who

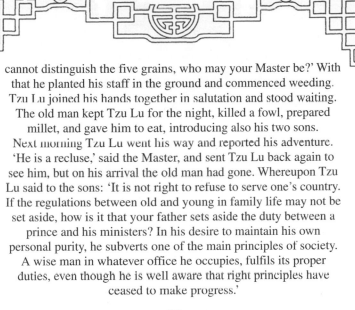

cannot distinguish the five grains, who may your Master be?' With
that he planted his staff in the ground and commenced weeding.
Tzu Lu joined his hands together in salutation and stood waiting.
The old man kept Tzu Lu for the night, killed a fowl, prepared
millet, and gave him to eat, introducing also his two sons.
Next morning Tzu Lu went his way and reported his adventure.
'He is a recluse,' said the Master, and sent Tzu Lu back again to
see him, but on his arrival the old man had gone. Whereupon Tzu
Lu said to the sons: 'It is not right to refuse to serve one's country.
If the regulations between old and young in family life may not be
set aside, how is it that your father sets aside the duty between a
prince and his ministers? In his desire to maintain his own
personal purity, he subverts one of the main principles of society.
A wise man in whatever office he occupies, fulfils its proper
duties, even though he is well aware that right principles have
ceased to make progress.'

The men noted for withdrawal into private life were Po I, Shu
Ch'i, Yü Chung, Yi Yi, Chu Chang, Hui of Liu-hsia, and
Shao Lien.
The Master observed: 'Those of them who would neither abate
their high purpose, nor abase themselves, it seems to me were Po I
and Shu Ch'i.[58] Concerning Hui of Liu-hsia and Shao Lien, while
they abated their high purpose and abased themselves, what they
said made for social order, and what they did hit the mark of what
men were anxious about: and that is all. Concerning Yü Chung and
Yi Yi, though in their seclusion they were immoderate in their
utterances, yet they sustained their personal purity, and their self-
immolation had weighty purpose.

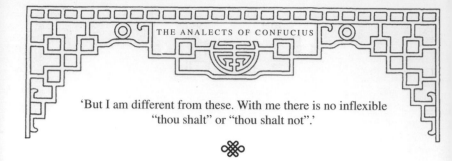

'But I am different from these. With me there is no inflexible
"thou shalt" or "thou shalt not".'

The Duke of Chou[59] addressing his son, the Duke of Lu, said:
'The wise prince does not neglect his relatives; nor does he cause
his chief ministers to be discontented at his not employing them;
he does not dismiss old servants from office without some grave
cause for it; nor does he expect one man to be capable
of everything.'

# BOOK XIX
## RECORDED SAYINGS OF SOME DISCIPLES

Tzu Chang said: 'A servant of the State, who in the presence of danger offers his life, whose first thought in presence of personal gain is whether it be right, whose first thought in sacrifice is reverence, and whose first thought in mourning is grief – he commands approval.'

Tzu Chang said: 'If a man possess virtue without its enlarging him, if he believe in truth but without steadfastness, how can you tell whether he has these qualities or not?'

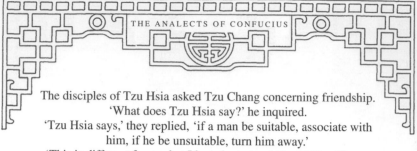

The disciples of Tzu Hsia asked Tzu Chang concerning friendship.
'What does Tzu Hsia say?' he inquired.
'Tzu Hsia says,' they replied, 'if a man be suitable, associate with
him, if he be unsuitable, turn him away.'
'This is different from what I have been taught,' said Tzu Chang.
'A wise man honours the worthy and tolerates all; he commends
the good and commiserates the incompetent. Am I a man of
exceptional worth? Then whom among men may I not tolerate?
Am I not a man of worth? Then others would be turning me away.
Why should there be this turning of others away then?'

Tzu Hsia said: 'Even the inferior arts certainly have their
attraction; but to go far into them involves a risk of their becoming
a hindrance to progress: so the wise man lets them alone.'

Tzu Hsia said: 'He who day by day finds out where he is
deficient, and who month by month never forgets that in
which he has become proficient, may truly be called a lover
of learning.'

Tzu Hsia said : 'Broad culture and a steady will, earnest
investigation and personal reflection – virtue is to be
found therein.'

Tzu Hsia said: 'As the various craftsmen dwell in their workshops that they may do their work effectively, so the Wise Man applies himself to study that he may carry his wisdom to perfection.'

Tzu Hsia said: 'The inferior man always embellishes his mistakes.'

Tzu Hsia said: 'The Wise Man varies from three aspects. Seen from a distance he appears stern; when approached he proves gracious; as you listen to him you find him decided in opinion.'

Tzu Hsia said: 'The Wise Man obtains the people's confidence before imposing burdens on them, for without confidence they will think themselves oppressed. He also obtains the confidence of his prince before pointing out his errors, for before obtaining such confidence his prince would deem himself aspersed.'

Tzu Hsia said: 'He who does not overstep the threshold in the major virtues, may have liberty of egress and ingress in the minor ones.'

Tzu Hsia said: 'The occupant of office when his duties are finished

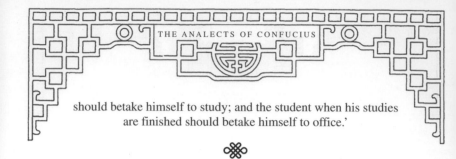

should betake himself to study; and the student when his studies are finished should betake himself to office.'

Tzu Yu remarked: 'My friend Chang [Tzu Chang] does things hardly possible to others, but he is not yet perfect in virtue.'

Tseng Tzu said: 'What a stately manner Chang puts on! It must be hard to live the perfect life alongside him.'

Tseng Tzu said: 'I have heard the Master say: "Though a man may never before have shown what was in him, surely he will do so when he mourns his parents."'

Tseng Tzu said: 'I have heard the Master observe that the filial piety of Meng Chuang Tzu[60] might in other particulars be possible to other men, but his unaltered maintenance of his father's servants, and of his father's administration – these they would hardly find possible.'

When the Chief of the Meng family appointed Yang Fu[61] as chief criminal judge, the latter came to ask advice of Tseng Tzu who

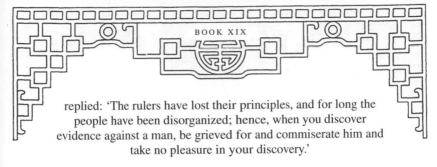

replied: 'The rulers have lost their principles, and for long the people have been disorganized; hence, when you discover evidence against a man, be grieved for and commiserate him and take no pleasure in your discovery.'

Tzu Kung said: 'The transgressions of the Wise Man are like eclipses of the sun or moon. When he transgresses all men look at him. When he recovers all men look up to him.'

Kung-sun Ch'ao of Wei once inquired of Tzu Kung: 'From whom did Chung Ni [Confucius] get his learning?' 'The doctrines of Wen and Wu[62] have never yet fallen to the ground,' replied Tzu Kung, 'but have remained amongst men. Gifted men have kept in mind their nobler principles, while others not so gifted have kept in mind the minor, so that nowhere have the doctrines of Wen and Wu been absent. From whom then, could our Master not learn? And, moreover, what need was there for him to have a regular teacher?'

Shu-sun Wu-shu,[63] talking to the high officers at Court, remarked: 'Tzu Kung is a superior man to Chung Ni [Confucius].' Tzu-fu Ching-po took and told this to Tzu Kung, who replied: 'One might illustrate the position with the boundary wall of a building. As to my wall, it only reaches to the shoulder, and with a peep you may see whatever is of value in the house and home. The Master's wall rises fathoms high, and unless you find the gate and go inside, you

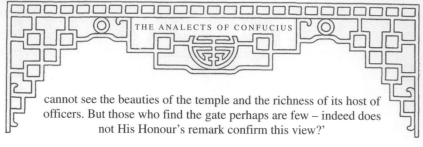

cannot see the beauties of the temple and the richness of its host of officers. But those who find the gate perhaps are few – indeed does not His Honour's remark confirm this view?'

Shu-sun Wu-shu having spoken disparagingly of Chung Ni, Tzu Kung observed: 'There is no use in doing that, for Chung Ni cannot be disparaged. The excellences of others are mounds and hillocks, which may nevertheless be climbed over, but Chung Ni! He is the sun, the moon, which there is no way of climbing over; and though a man may desire to cut himself off from them, what harm does he do to the sun or moon? He only shows that he has no idea of proportion.'

Ch'en Tzu Chin once said to Tzu Kung: 'You are too modest, Sir. How can Chung Ni be considered superior to you?'
'An educated man,' replied Tzu Kung, 'for a single expression is often deemed wise, and for a single expression is often deemed foolish; hence one should not be heedless in what one says. The impossibility of equalling our Master is like the impossibility of scaling a ladder and ascending to the skies. Were our Master to obtain control of a country, then, as has been said, "He raises his people and they stand; he leads them, and they follow; he gives them tranquillity and multitudes resort to him; he brings his influence to bear on them and they live in harmony; his life is glorious and his death bewailed" – how is it possible for him to be equalled?'

# BOOK XX
## CONCERNING RIGHT GOVERNMENT

Yao[64] said: 'O, thou Shun! The celestial lineage rests in thy person. Faithfully hold to the golden mean. Should the land become lean, Heaven's bounties will forever end towards you.' And Shun in like terms charged Yü.

T'ang said: 'I thy child Li, Dare to use a black ox, And dare clearly to state to Thee, O Most August and Sovereign God, That the sinner I dare not spare, Nor keep Thy ministers, O God, in obscurity, As Thy heart, O God, discerns. If I have sinned, Let it not concern the country; If my country has sinned, Let the sin rest on me.'

Wu of Chou conferred great largesses, the good being enriched. 'Although,' said he, 'the tyrant Chou had his host of princes

121

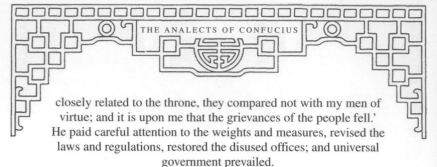

closely related to the throne, they compared not with my men of virtue; and it is upon me that the grievances of the people fell.'
He paid careful attention to the weights and measures, revised the laws and regulations, restored the disused offices; and universal government prevailed.
He re-established states that had been extinguished, restored the lines of broken succession, called to office men who had exiled themselves; and all the people gave him their hearts. What he laid stress on were the people's food, mourning for the dead, and sacrifices. By his magnanimity he won all, by his good faith he gained the people's confidence, by his diligence he achieved his ends, and by his justice all were gratified.

Tzu Chang inquired of Confucius, saying, 'How should a man act to achieve the proper administration of government?' The Master replied: 'Let him honour the five good and banish the four bad rules; then he will be a worthy administrator.'
'What is meant by the five good rules?' asked Tzu Chang. 'That the ruler,' replied the Master, 'be beneficent without expending the public revenue, that he exact service without arousing dissatisfaction, that his desires never degenerate to greed, that he be dignified but without disdain, and that he be commanding but not domineering.'
'What is meant by beneficence without expenditure?' asked Tzu Chang. The Master replied: 'To benefit the people by the development of their natural resources; is not this a public benefaction without expense to the revenue? If he selects suitable works to exact from them – who then will be dissatisfied? If his desires are for the good of others, and he secures it, how can he be

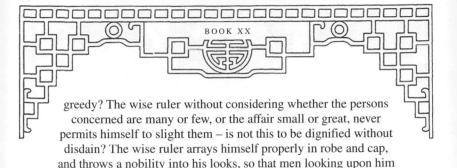

greedy? The wise ruler without considering whether the persons concerned are many or few, or the affair small or great, never permits himself to slight them – is not this to be dignified without disdain? The wise ruler arrays himself properly in robe and cap, and throws a nobility into his looks, so that men looking upon him in his dignity stand in awe of him – and is not this commanding without being domineering?'

'What is the meaning of the four bad rules?' asked Tzu Chang. The Master replied, 'Putting men to death without having taught them their duty – which may be called cruelty; expecting the completion of works when no warning has been given – which may be called oppression; remissness in ordering and then demand for instant performance   which may be called robbery; and likewise, when giving rewards to men, offering them in grudging fashion – which may be called being merely an official.'

The Master said: 'He who does not know the divine law cannot become a noble man. He who does not know the laws of right conduct cannot form his character. He who does not know the force of words, cannot know men.'

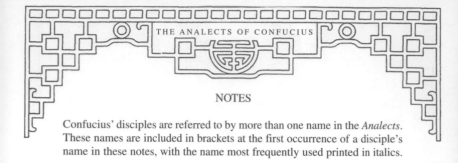

## NOTES

Confucius' disciples are referred to by more than one name in the *Analects*. These names are included in brackets at the first occurrence of a disciple's name in these notes, with the name most frequently used printed in italics.

### BOOK I

1. Yu (Yu Juo, Yu Tzu, *Tzu Yu*); Tseng (Tseng Shen, Shen, *Tseng Tzu*); *Tzu Hsia* (Pu Shang, Shang); *Tzu Ch'in* (Ch'en K'ang), *Tzu Kung* (Tuan-mu Tzu, Tz'u): disciples of Confucius.

### BOOK II

2. The Odes or *Shih Ching* are said to have been compiled by Confucius himself.

3. Meng I Tzu (Meng Sun): minister of Lu prior to Confucius' exile. Meng Wu Po: son of Meng I Tzu.

4. *Fan Ch'ih* (Fan Hsu); *Tzu Yu* (Yen Yen); *Hui* (Yen Hui, Yen Yüan); *Tzu Chang* (Tuan-sun Shih): disciples of Confucius. Hui was Confucius' favourite disciple.

5. Duke Ai: duke of Lu when Confucius returned from exile.

6. Chi K'ang Tzu (K'ang Tzu): minister to Duke Ai of Lu, he recalled Confucius and his disciples from exile.

### BOOK III

7. A comment on the arrogance of Chi in adopting an Imperial rite.

8. *Lin Fang*: disciple of Confucius.

9. The Chou dynasty was founded by Duke Wen of Chou – sometimes called King Wen – who served as regent during the minority of his nephew, later King Wu. Confucius considered Wen the ideal of a good ruler.

10. Duke Ting of Lu: Confucius served as his minister before the exile.

11. *Tsai Wo* (Tsai Yü, Yü): disciple of Confucius.

12. Shao (Succession) and Wen (Overthrow) were musical forms associated respectively with Shun and Wu, two rulers of ancient China. The former came to the throne through succession, the latter by overthrowing his rivals.

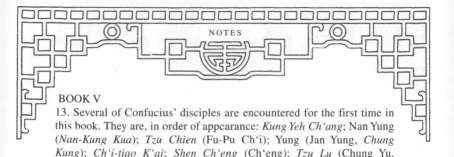

### BOOK V

13. Several of Confucius' disciples are encountered for the first time in this book. They are, in order of appearance: *Kung Yeh Ch'ang*; Nan Yung (*Nan-Kung Kua*); *Tzu Chien* (Fu-Pu Ch'i); Yung (Jan Yung, *Chung Kung*); *Ch'i-tiao K'ai*; *Shen Ch'eng* (Ch'eng); *Tzu Lu* (Chung Yu, Chi Lu).

14. K'ung Tzu: a Counsellor of Wei. Given the posthumous title 'Wen' (meaning 'cultured') and referred to in later books of the *Analects* by his full name of Kung-shu Wen-tzu.

15. The people named in Book V from here onwards are ministers or officers of state, apart from one paragraph which concerns disciples of Confucius.

### BOOK VI

16. *Jan Ch'iu* (Jan Yu, Ch'iu): disciple of Confucius.

17. Yao and Shun: legendary rulers of ancient China, renowned for their wisdom, moral character and benevolence.

### BOOK VII

18. The *Book of Changes*: also known as the *I Ching*, one of the classic texts of ancient China, is variously described as a book of divination, philosophy or cosmological processes. According to tradition, Confucius wrote a commentary on it.

19. *Kung-hsi Hua* (Kung-hsi Ch'ih, Ch'ih): disciple of Confucius.

### BOOK VIII

20. Meng Ching Tzu: son of Meng Wu Po (*see* note 3).

21. Shun and Yü: legendary emperors from the 23rd century BCE.

### BOOK IX

22. When Confucius came to K'uang during the exile, he found himself in danger because he was mistaken for somebody else.

23: Lao (Chi'in Chang): disciple of Confucius.

24: The hypothetical 'jewel' to which Tzu Kung refers is Confucius' teaching.

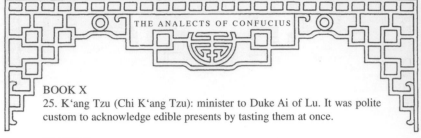

## BOOK X

25. K'ang Tzu (Chi K'ang Tzu): minister to Duke Ai of Lu. It was polite custom to acknowledge edible presents by tasting them at once.

## BOOK XI

26. Confucius is referring back to his period in exile and the disciples who were with him then. Mentioned for the first time here are *Min Tzu Ch'ien* (Min Tzu); Jan Niu (Jan Keng, *Po Niu*); *Jan Yu*.

27. Yu = Tzu Lu. He trained as a soldier and was killed in battle, fighting for his lord.

28. Shih = Tzu Chang; Shang = Tzu Hsia (Pu Shang).

29. Ch'ai = Kao Ch'ai (Tzu Kao); Shen = Tseng Tzu (Tseng Shen); Shih = Tzu Chang; Yu = Tzu Lu. Confucius is describing the character of these disciples when they first came to him.

30. Hui = Yen Yüan; T'zu = Tzu Kung.

31. Chi Tzu-jan: younger brother of the minister Chi K'ang Tzu (*see* note 25). They were thinking of doing away with their prince.

## BOOK XII

32. Ssu-ma Niu's brother, Huan T'ui, had tried to kill Confucius.

33. Chi Tzu-Ch'eng: an official who questions the value of art and self-refinement.

## BOOK XIII

34. She: a small state.

35. Chü-fu: a city in Lu.

## BOOK XIV

36. Hsien (Yüan Hsien, *Yüan Ssu*): disciple of Confucius.

37. Prince I, Ao, Yü and Chi: legendary figures from antiquity. Prince I and Ao were famed for their individual heroic feats whereas Yü and Chi were noted for their contribution to wider society: because Yü successfully tamed China's Great Flood, the legendary emperor Shun considered him a worthy successor and abdicated in his favour; in turn, Yü appointed his son Chi as his successor and thus established China's first recorded dynasty, the Hsia dynasty.

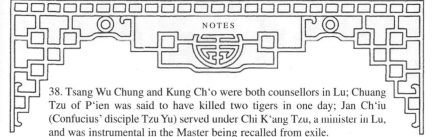

38. Tsang Wu Chung and Kung Ch'o were both counsellors in Lu; Chuang Tzu of P'ien was said to have killed two tigers in one day; Jan Ch'iu (Confucius' disciple Tzu Yu) served under Chi K'ang Tzu, a minister in Lu, and was instrumental in the Master being recalled from exile.

39. Kung-shu Wen-tzu: an official in Wei, who was also a philosopher (*see* note 14).

40. Duke Ling of Wei: an unprincipled ruler who retained his throne only through the proficiency of his ministers. Chi K'ang Tzu: a minister in Lu.

41. Chü Po Yü: an official in Wei and former disciple of Confucius.

42. Wei-sheng Mou: an elderly recluse. Ch'iu = Confucius.

43. Kung-po Liao: a disciple of Confucius. Chi-sun = Chi K'ang Tzu, the Lu minister. Tzu-fu Ching-po: a prominent official in Lu.

44. Kao Tsung: emperor of the Shang dynasty.

45. Yao and Shun: legendary emperors.

46. Yüan Jang: an elderly scoundrel, said to have been an old friend of Confucius.

## BOOK XV

47. Yü and Chü Po Yü: officials in Wei (*see also* note 41).

48. The Hsia calendar mirrored the harmonious cosmological relationship of the heavens, earth and humankind; the state carriage of Yin was a simple wooden carriage, devoid of ornamentation; the cap of Chou was used for sacred rites; the gestures of the Shao dances were stately and ordered; the songs of Cheng were considered frivolous by Confucius.

49. In Confucius' time, the musical profession was open only to those who were blind.

## BOOK XVI

50. Po Yü: Confucius' son.

## BOOK XVII

51. Tzu Yu (Yen Yen): disciple of Confucius and administrator in Wu where he had worked hard to put in to effect the Master's principles of government. He mistakenly interpreted Confucius' playful remark as a criticism of his zeal.

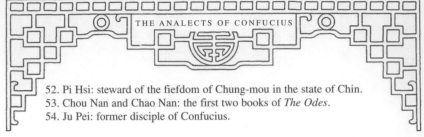

52. Pi Hsi: steward of the fiefdom of Chung-mou in the state of Chin.
53. Chou Nan and Chao Nan: the first two books of *The Odes*.
54. Ju Pei: former disciple of Confucius.

## BOOK XVIII

55. Chou: a brutal tyrant, last of the Shang emperors, 1153–1122BCE. Pi Kan and the viscounts of Wei and Chi were his relatives, yet when they tried to persuade Chou to change his ways he punished them.
56. Hui of Liu-hsia: an incorruptible judge.
57. Ch'ang Chü and Chieh Ni: two recluses.
58. Po I and Shu Ch'i: two princes who withdrew from court and died of starvation rather than betray their principles. Hui Liu-hsia, *see* note 56.
59. Duke of Chou: acted as regent for his son, the Duke of Lu.

## BOOK XIX

60. Meng Chuang Tzu: a minister of Lu.
61. Yang Fu: a disciple of Tseng Tzu (disciple of Confucius).
62. Wen and Wu: a reference to Kings Wen and Wu, founders of the Chou dynasty (*see* note 9).
63. Shu-sun Wu-shu: a high official of Lu.

## BOOK XX

64. The first section of this book records sayings and actions attributed to the founders of the great dynasties.